**PLAYBACK+**
Speed • Pitch • Balance • Loop

Transcriptions • Lessons • Bios • Photos

# 25 GREAT FLUTE SOLOS

Featuring Pop Music Flutists, including Ian Anderson, Katisse Buckingham, Tony Iommi, Bob Messenger, David Shostac, Collin Tilton, Ann Wilson, and Many More

**By Eric J. Morones**

To access audio visit:
**www.halleonard.com/mylibrary**

Enter Code
1951-2153-5459-7531

Cover Photo Credits:
Ian Anderson © David Warner Ellis / Getty, Katisse Buckingham © Ian Barling, Walter Parazaider © Larry Marano / Getty, Ann Wilson © Al Pereira / Getty, Ray Thomas © Pictorial Press Ltd / Alamy Stock Photo, Jerry Eubanks © Tom Hill / Getty

ISBN 978-1-4950-0873-3

**HAL•LEONARD®**
CORPORATION

7777 W. BLUEMOUND RD. P.O. BOX 13819 MILWAUKEE, WI 53213

Visit Hal Leonard Online at
**www.halleonard.com**

# Preface

*25 Great Flute Solos* is a collection of some of the most renowned and significant flute solos/melodies ever recorded. Compared to saxophone or guitar solos, flute solos are uncommon in pop music. (Extensive investigation was required just to find these 25!) But some of these songs and melodies are classics: famous, recognizable, and ones you could hear almost anywhere in the world. Others may become the new standard in flute solo repertoire. And for the person who has always wanted to learn these famous flute melodies ("licks"), it's all here.

These solos/songs were chosen using various criteria: popularity, acquirable publishing rights, musical content, and familiarity. Others were chosen for being worthy, if unknown, solos. Some are short and easy. Some are difficult. Some require advanced flute chops, while others are at a level that even a beginner can attempt.

Exhaustive research was done to provide accurate biographical material, as well as vital information about the solos, equipment, recording, musicians, and players. In some instances, data could not be found or was otherwise unavailable.

A few solos are performed on piccolo. If you don't own one, playing the excerpts on a C flute will work just as well. Know that the music will sound an octave lower than the recording.

# About the Online Audio

There are two online audio versions for each solo: 1) a demo track with the solo flute; 2) a backing track without the solo flute. These allow you to hear how the solo sounds, and provide an opportunity to play it along with the rhythm track. The time code shown at the start of each transcribed excerpt indicates the point where the solo begins on the source recording. Though the audio tracks attempt to replicate the original performances, there is no substitute for the real thing. In most instances, you can find these online, so please search them out and listen.

The music on the audio tracks is performed by:

| | |
|---|---|
| Eric J. Morones | flute, piccolo, saxophones, keyboards |
| Hiro Morozumi | keyboards |
| Andy Alt | guitar |
| Ross Schodek | bass |
| Dave Johnstone | drums |

Orchestral arrangement of "Somewhere in Time" by Gordy Haab
Produced by Eric J. Morones
Recorded and mixed by Wesley Switzer at Milestone Studios, Los Angeles, California

Thank you to Jeff Schroedl and Hal Leonard Corporation, to the wonderful musicians on this project, and to the amazing flutists who played these great solos for us to learn.

# Contents

# Plas Johnson

© Frans Schellekens / Getty

**Plas Johnson**

> *"I've been very fortunate. I guess I had good judgment about what to play, and what they wanted."*
>
> –Plas Johnson

Call him the "Pink Panther" if you want, but you should just call him the Hollywood studio "Legend."

Plas Johnson was born on July 21, 1931 in Donaldsville, Louisiana. His father and mother both played piano, and his father also played alto sax. Plas first started playing soprano sax at age 12, moving over to tenor sax at age 15. In his late teens, he formed the popular Johnson Brothers Combo with his pianist brother Ray, working around New Orleans and backing visiting artists like Big Joe Turner and Wynonie Harris. In 1951, Johnson left New Orleans to go on the road with the Charles Brown Blues Band. This experience taught him to improvise and to play jazz and R&B solos. After later serving in the Army, he moved to Los Angeles. There, Plas attended the Westlake School of Music for a year and a half, until he got too busy with record dates. Playing soulful sax solos as well as woodwinds, he become a regular session sideman and soloist during Capitol Records' busy recording years. In 1963, Plas became the official "Pink Panther," recording the famous Henry Mancini composition and putting his musical stamp on it. He also played on another Mancini hit, "Peter Gunn," and worked with such diverse artists as Nat King Cole, Frank Sinatra, Frank Zappa, Little Richard, Peggy Lee, the Platters, Duane Eddy, Ella Fitzgerald, Marvin Gaye, Tina Turner, Screamin' Jay Hawkins, and the Beach Boys.

Johnson joined *The Merv Griffin Show* band in 1970, remaining there for 15 years. (The ensemble included an all-star line-up of prominent instrumentalists like Ray Brown, Herb Ellis, Jake Hanna, Benny Powell, and Jack Sheldon.) With Harry "Sweets" Edison, Plas recorded "The Odd Couple Theme." Across the years, he has released the solo albums *Hot, Blue & Saxy*, *This Must Be Plas*, *Evening Delight*, *Christmas in Hollywood*, and *Keep That Groove Going!* Today, Plas continues to record and perform live dates.

Robert James Byrd was born on July 1, 1928 in Fort Worth, Texas. He moved to Los Angeles at age 15. As a member of the R&B group the Hollywood Flames, he used the stage name Bobby Day to perform and record. After several years with little success, in 1957 Day formed his own band, the Satellites. With classics like "Over and Over" (the Dave Clark Five), "Little Bitty Pretty One" (popularized by Thurston Harris in 1957), and the 1958 version of "Rockin' Robin," he became known as a hit songwriter. Day died of cancer on July 27, 1990 in Los Angeles.

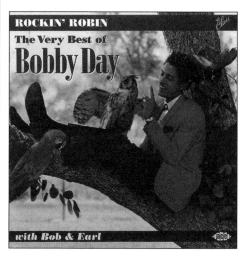

# How to Play It

"Rockin' Robin" (originally titled "Rock-In Robin") has been recorded by many artists and was a No. 2 hit for the Jackson 5 in 1972. The song was penned by R&B songwriter Leon René (under the pseudonym Jimmie Thomas), who also wrote the classics "Gloria" and "Boogie Woogie Santa Claus." The song "Rockin' Robin" became a *Billboard* Hot 100 No. 2 hit (No. 1 on the R&B charts), selling over one million copies, and was awarded a gold record.

This brief solo is reminiscent of the whistling an American robin. It is scored for piccolo in a standard 12-bar blues form. (If you don't own a piccolo, which is an octave higher than the C flute, you can play it "as is." It will sound an octave lower than the piccolo.) The excerpt begins on a high D with a *flutter tongue*.* Be sure to use enough air to get the flutter started – this is the hardest part. You may want to start blowing before the note is supposed to sound, as getting the flutter to work properly takes at least a beat.

Notice that the solo is in the highest octave of the piccolo, which is often shrill and loud. It is also difficult to maintain good pitch, though Plas Johnson has no problem doing just that. Use enough air to keep the pitches up where they need to be. The solo is played with a nice variety in articulation, so pay attention to all notated slurs, staccatos and accents.

*Flutter tonguing is an advanced flute technique performed by rolling your "Rs" with your tongue while you play (such as used in spoken languages like Spanish). It gives the sound/note a harsh, growly, aggressive tone, but requires a great deal more air.

"Rockin' Robin" is in the public domain. It is not under copyright restrictions, so you can create your own arrangements and recordings without having to pay royalties.

## Vital Stats

**Flute player:** Plas Johnson
**Song:** "Rockin' Robin"
**Album:** *Rockin' Robin*
**Age at time of recording:** 27

# Roland Kirk

We can thank *Austin Powers: International Man of Mystery* for bringing this Quincy Jones classic back to the mainstream!

"Rahsaan" Roland Kirk was born Ronald Theodore Kirk on August 7, 1935 in Columbus, Ohio. He went blind at age two as a result of poor medical treatment. He started playing the bugle and trumpet, later learning the clarinet and C-melody sax. By age 15, he was playing tenor sax professionally in R&B bands. His first recording, *Triple Threat*, was released in 1956. In 1960, he moved to Chicago, then spent three months in Germany touring with Charles Mingus. Preferring to lead his own bands, Kirk rarely performed as a sideman, though he recorded with arranger Quincy Jones and drummer Roy Haynes.

Always the forward thinker, Kirk began making his own instruments and constructing three of his saxes so they could be played simultaneously. He played the nose whistle, flute, piccolo, harmonica, "trumpophone" (a trumpet with a soprano sax mouthpiece), and "slidesophone" (a small trombone or slide trumpet, also with a sax mouthpiece) that he invented. Considered a gimmick by many, Kirk's playing of multiple instruments nevertheless was serious and innovative. By 1963, he had mastered circular breathing, a technique that enabled him to play long notes and passages without pausing for breath.

Kirk added "Rahsaan" to his name after hearing it in a dream in 1970. He also switched two letters in his first name to become Roland. As an activist, Kirk lead the Jazz and People's Movement, a group devoted to opening up new opportunities

> *"People talk about freedom, but the blues is still one of the freest things you can play. If you know the changes, you can take them anywhere you want to go."*
> –Roland Kirk

George Konig / Stringer / Getty

**Roland Kirk**

for jazz musicians. In 1975, he suffered a paralyzing stroke that impaired movement on one side of his body. He modified his instruments to enable him to play with one arm and continued to perform and record. Following a performance in Bloomington, Indiana, Kirk died from a second stroke on December 5, 1977.

Quincy Jones is one of the 20th century's most famous and creative musicians. Quincy Delight Jones Jr. was born on March 14, 1933 in Chicago, Illinois. His family moved to Seattle when he was young. He soon found his love for music while in enrolled in grade school, where he met his future friend and music legend, Ray Charles. Jones began playing the trombone in band, then switched to trumpet. In 1951, he attended Berklee College of Music on a scholarship, eventually dropping out to tour with Lionel Hampton's band as a trumpeter and conductor. After living in Europe for several years, he returned to New York in 1954. There, he composed, arranged, and recorded for artists such as Duke Ellington, Ray Charles, Sarah Vaughan, Count Basie, Dinah Washington, LeVern Baker, and Big Maybell. He also held an executive position at Mercury Records.

In 1963, he won his first Grammy Award for his Count Basie arrangement of "I Can't Stop Loving You." The next year, he composed music for *The Pawnbroker*, the first of nearly 40 film scores. By the mid-1960s he was conductor and arranger for Frank Sinatra's orchestra, arranging one of Sinatra's most memorable songs, "Fly Me to the Moon." As well as releasing albums under his own name,

Jones scored several films, including *In the Heat of the Night*, *Jigsaw*, *The Italian Job*, and music for the TV mini-series *Roots* (1977). The next year, while working on the movie *The Wiz*, he met superstar Michael Jackson, sparking a musical friendship that produced some of the greatest pop albums ever – including the monumental bestselling album *Thriller*. Today, the record-breaking disc has sold more than 100 million copies worldwide.

Jones was inducted into the Rock and Roll Hall of Fame in 2013. With 79 Grammy nominations (27 wins), an Emmy, and nearly every award imaginable, he has established himself as one of popular music's geniuses.

# How to Play It

"Soul Bossa Nova" was written by Quincy Jones and released on his 1962 *Big Band Bossa Nova* album. The song is used in a number soundtracks, most recently the Austin Powers films. It features piccolos and a soulful flute solo by Kirk. The famous melody is written for two piccolos in harmony. However, if no piccolos are available, feel free to play it as written on flutes, knowing it will sound an octave lower when practicing. Listen closely to the intonation on the unison notes, or consider having one piccolo drop out until the duet part

comes back. It's difficult to play unison piccolo notes in tune.

After the famous piccolo melody, Kirk's growly, soulful solo starts on the solo break at measure 29 with a high hummed F. Humming while playing creates an aggressive, growly, feedback effect similar to flutter tonguing. This technique also takes a great deal more air and a relaxed throat. When learning to do this, start humming first, and then blow the note. The hard part is doing both simultaneously. It's a good idea to start out with a mid-range note and progress to the higher octave used in this solo. Once you have the hang of it, hum while playing the entire excerpt.

## Vital Stats

**Flute player:** Roland Kirk
**Song:** "Soul Bossa Nova"
**Album:** *Big Band Bossa Nova*
**Age at time of recording:** 27

# Thomas "Beans" Bowles

Courtesy of the E. Azalia Hackley Collection of African Americans in the Performing Arts, Detroit Public Library

Thomas "Beans" Bowles

of a Motown session band called the Funk Brothers.

It was Bowles who suggested that Motown Records founder Berry Gordy Jr. put all his young artists on a bus to tour as the Motown Revue. With Beans as the road manager, the "Motor Town Special" (renamed the "Motor Town Revue" in April 1963) toured across the USA featuring many Motown artists. Bowles later toured with such musicians as Illinois Jacquet, Bill Doggett, and Lloyd Price. He allegedly composed the Stevie Wonder song "Fingertips Part I," but never received his share of the song's royalties. In his post-Motown years, he was director of the Graystone Jazz Museum Orchestra in Detroit. Bowles died on January 29, 2000, after battling prostate cancer.

Marvin Gaye was born Marvin Pentz Gay Jr. on April 2, 1939. Gaye helped shape the sound of Motown in the 1960s, first as an in-house session player and later as a solo artist – with hits like "How Sweet It Is (To Be Loved By You)," "I Heard It Through the Grapevine," "Pride and Joy," and "Stubborn Kind of Fellow." In 1971, he released his bestselling concept album, *What's Going On*, which was ranked No. 6 on *Rolling Stone* magazine's 2003 list of the 500 Greatest Albums of All Time. In 1982, Gaye released the Grammy Award-winning hit "Sexual Healing" and its parent album *Midnight Love*. On April 1, 1984, he was fatally shot during an argument with his father, Marvin Gay Sr.

"Stubborn Kind of Fellow" is just one of the many classic songs written and performed by Marvin Gaye. It features the flute of Thomas "Beans" Bowles.

Thomas "Beans" Bowles was born Harold Thomas Bowles on May 7, 1926 in South Bend, Indiana. Nicknamed "String Bean" (later "Beans") because

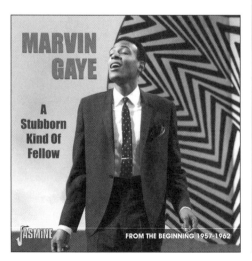

of his lanky, six-foot five-inch frame, he started first on clarinet at age nine, and by 16 was working professionally as a saxophonist. In 1944, he went to Detroit, playing in many jazz bars with the likes of Billie Holiday and Billy Eckstine. He attended Wayne State University, but soon dropped out to play with the U.S. Navy Band. In the 1960s, Bowles led a Detroit band called the Swinging Dashikis, which often backed up Motown acts. He became the Temptations' first manager, as well as musical director for Smokey Robinson & the Miracles, and the Four Tops. A versatile musician, Bowles played on Gaye's "What's Goin' On," the Supremes' hit "Baby Love," "Do You Love Me" by the Contours, and Martha and the Vandellas' "Heat Wave." At that time, he was also an integral part

*"I sing about life."*

–Marvin Gaye

Since his death, many institutions have posthumously bestowed Gaye with awards and other honors, including the Grammy Lifetime Achievement Award. He was inducted into the Rock and Roll Hall of Fame in 1987 and into the Rhythm and Blues Music Hall of Fame in 2014.

# How to Play It

"Stubborn Kind of Fellow" was co-written by Gaye and William "Mickey" Stevenson. It was Gaye's first hit single, reaching No. 46 on the *Billboard* Hot 100 (No. 8 on R&B chart) in late 1962.

This classic eight-bar solo by Bowles contains a few tricky spots. The bebop-like lick in measure 3 will take practice, as it goes by quickly. Work it out slowly, gradually increasing the tempo over time. Measure 7 is basically a flurry of high notes with no real notation. You can either play the notes and rhythms written (I would suggest an octave higher), or simply articulate some fast high notes within the A♭ chord and you'll be set.

Then we come to the flutter-tongued high G and A♭ in bar 8. Take a deep breath and flutter through the A♭ if possible, leading into the 16th notes. Keep a relaxed throat and let the air flow as quickly as possible. Then use a light tongue to keep the 16th notes clean, while keeping the air flowing. Try not to take a breath in between the half note and 16ths.

## Vital Stats

**Flute player:** Thomas "Beans" Bowles

**Song:** "Stubborn Kind of Fellow"

**Album:** *That Stubborn Kind of Fellow*

**Age at time of recording:** 36

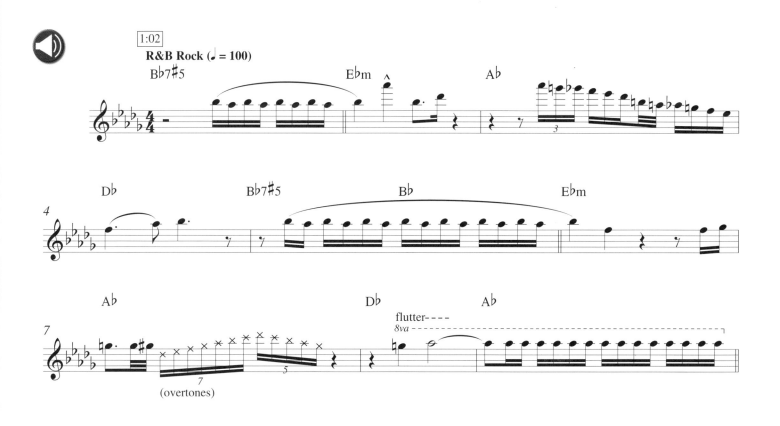

## Bud Shank

© Gilles Petard / Getty

**Bud Shank**

Bud Shank adds the perfect jazz influence on this hit for the Mamas and the Papas.

Clifford Everett "Bud" Shank Jr. was born on May 27, 1926 in Dayton, Ohio. Growing up on a farm, he began playing the clarinet at age ten after hearing Artie Shaw and Benny Goodman on the radio. At age 12, he started the saxophone. He studied music at the University of North Carolina, leaving during his third year to go on the road. His first musical break was playing tenor sax with Charlie Barnett in 1946.

Heading to Los Angeles in 1949, and now playing alto sax, Shank performed with Stan Kenton and Chet Baker and started doing studio work. Playing in Kenton's Innovations in Modern Music

Band helped boost Shank's jazz world profile, leading to a solo jazz career in the early 1950s. He helped develop the West Coast "Cool" alto sound, along with other altoists Paul Desmond and Lee Konitz. He soon teamed up with Brazilian acoustic guitarist Laurindo Almeida and had success with the group LA 4. In 1962, he fused jazz with Indian traditions in a collaboration with Indian composer and sitar-player Ravi Shankar. He was a member of ensembles as diverse as the Royal Philharmonic Orchestra, the New American Orchestra, the Gerald Wilson Big Band, Stan Kenton's Neophonic Orchestra, and the Duke Ellington Orchestra.

After playing the flute as a second instrument over the years with much success, he dropped it during the 1980s to become purely an alto saxophonist. In 2005, he formed the Bud Shank Big Band in Los Angeles to celebrate the 40th anniversary of Stan Kenton's Neophonic Orchestra.

A documentary film, *Bud Shank: Against the Tide – Portrait of a Jazz Legend*, was produced and directed by Graham Carter of Jazzed Media and released by Jazzed Media as a DVD in 2008. Shank died on April 2, 2009, of a pulmonary embolism at his home in Tucson, Arizona.

The Mamas and the Papas were a major part of the Southern California pop scene in the mid-to-late '60s. With the mix of male voices John Phillips and Denny Doherty, and female voices Cass Elliot and Michelle Phillips, their folk-pop songs delivered with lush harmonies became a staple of that era's music.

The group formed out of the New Folk movement of the late '50s and early '60s. After calling themselves the Magic Circle for a short time, they took the name the Mamas and the Papas, signing to Lou Adler's Dunhill label. Their debut album, *If You Can Believe Your Eyes and Ears*, stands as a peak moment in the West Coast vocal-group sound. A string of hit singles followed with "California Dreamin,'" "Monday Monday," "I Saw Her Again," and "Creque Alley." Their amazing blend, with its intricate harmonies and vocal interweaving, prompted *Life* magazine to proclaim them "the most inventive pop musical group and first really new vocal sound since the Beatles."

Sadly, the band broke up in 1968 due to disagreements. They reunited briefly in 1971 to meet a contractual obligation, but soon disbanded to pursue solo careers. Cass "Mama Cass" Elliot was the most successful of the members; she died of a heart attack on July 29, 1974.

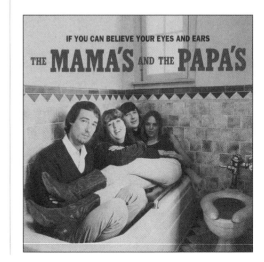

IF YOU CAN BELIEVE YOUR EYES AND EARS

THE **MAMA'S** AND THE **PAPA'S**

# How to Play It

*"You can't be the best flute player and the best alto saxophone player, no matter how hard you try. There are not enough hours in the day."*

–Bud Shank

"California Dreamin" was one of the Mamas and the Papas' biggest hits. It was written by John Phillips and Michelle Phillips and was first recorded by Barry McGuire. The group released their version as a single in 1965. The song is No. 89 in *Rolling Stone*'s list of the 500 Greatest Songs of All Time, and has been covered by many artists, including the Beach Boys. It was certified as a Gold Record (single) by the Recording Industry Association of America (RIAA) in June 1966 and was inducted into the Grammy Hall of Fame in 2001.

Shank begins with a beautifully rich, low-register line. Use warm, medium-speed vibrato with plenty of air to make sure the low C, C♯ and D are heard in measures 5–6. Keep your embouchure relaxed throughout.

At measure 9 you'll hear some jazz scoops and bends. There are two ways to accomplish these. Experiment to determine which works better for you.

1. Relax the lower lip and lower your air into the mouthpiece to get a lower pitch. Then, "lip" it up. This method is the preferred one, as it allows a fuller tone.

2. Relax the lower lip and roll your head joint in and out to change the pitch. This method produces a smaller tone, but is the easier of the two.

## Vital Stats

**Flute player:** Bud Shank
**Song:** "California Dreamin"
**Album:** *If You Can Believe Your Eyes and Ears*
**Age at time of recording:** 39

**Words and Music by John Phillips and Michelle Phillips**
Copyright © 1965 UNIVERSAL MUSIC CORP.
Copyright Renewed
All Rights Reserved   Used by Permission

# Ray Thomas

*"I never took a lesson in my life and just taught myself. I've got a few bad habits I can't rid myself of after all this time – like on the fingering and how to hold the flute. I don't do it correctly."*

–Ray Thomas

**Ray Thomas**

The Moody Blues are known for their mystical, psychedelic music. Band member Ray Thomas's flute only made their hit "Nights in White Satin" more beautiful. Selling over 70 million albums worldwide, and with 14 platinum and gold discs, they basically patented the "concept" LP.

Raymond "Ray" Thomas was born on December 29, 1941 in Lickhill Manor, Stourport-on-Severn, England. His father sparked his musical interest when he taught Ray to play the harmonica at age nine. His inspiration to take up the flute came from one his grandfathers, who played the instrument. Ray joined the school choir at age ten, but left school a couple years later to become a tool-maker trainee. When he was 16, he went in search of a band to be a full-time musician.

In 1962, Thomas and keyboardist Mike Pinder formed the Krew Cats and decided to move to Hamburg, Germany to search for work. When that band broke up the next year, the two decided to put together a new group. Bandmates Thomas, bassist John Lodge, and Pinder were already in a group called El Riot & the Rebels. Looking for a new direction, they formed the Moody Blues in 1964 in Birmingham, England.

The group started out with R&B-based songs, but soon got into more experimental pop sounds. Thomas returned to the flute as his primary instrument, and his voice featured more prominently in their new music. He added "Another Morning" and "Twilight Time" to their growing repertoire of new, more adventurous songs, which were captured on their 1967 breakthrough album *Days of Future Passed*.

Their debut album, *The Magnificent Moodies*, featured their first hit, "Go Now!" It went to No. 1 on the U.K. singles charts (No. 10 on the U.S. *Billboard* Hot 100). Their hugely successful album *Days of Future Passed* became a landmark in the band's history. With its classical, orchestral feel, it featured the hit singles "Nights in White Satin" and "Tuesday Afternoon," with Thomas on flute. Their next album, *In Search of the Lost Chord*, abandoned the orchestra in favor of the Mellotron, which quickly became a part of their signature sound.

Having released dozens of songs since the 1960s, they experienced an unexpected resurgence with their 1986 hit "In Your Wildest Dreams." It peaked at No. 9 in the U.S., something that had not happened to a Moody Blues song since "Nights in White Satin" in 1972.

In the spring of 1997, PolyGram released remastered and upgraded versions of all seven of the group's classic late 1960s/early 1970s albums, with dramatically improved sound and new liner notes featuring recollections by the group members. They remain active and still tour extensively, with one member from

the original band from 1964 and two more from the 1967 lineup.

During the group's 1974 to 1978 hiatus, Thomas released a pair of solo albums, *From Mighty Oaks* and *Hopes, Wishes, Dreams*. These albums presented Thomas's singing, but not his playing. In 2002, Thomas retired from the Moody Blues.

## Vital Stats

**Flute player:** Ray Thomas
**Song:** "Nights in White Satin"
**Album:** *Days of Future Passed*
**Age at time of recording:** 26

# How to Play It

Band memeber Justin Hayward wrote the music and lyrics for "Nights in White Satin." The song reached No. 19 on the U.K. singles chart and No. 2 on the *Billboard* Hot 100. It earned a Gold certification for sales of a million copies. A Spanish version of the song, "Noches de Seda," was released at the same time. The song re-charted in the U.K. in late 1972, climbing to No. 9. There are two single versions of the song, both stripped of the orchestral and "Late Lament" poetry sections of the LP version. The London Festival Orchestra provided the symphonic accompaniment for the introduction. The orchestral sounds in the main body of the song were produced electronically by Mike Pinder's Mellotron keyboard.

This solo is a great showcase for traditional flute tone – clear and strong. Add some 16th-note vibrato to any note a quarter note or longer. Think classical flute. The high E at the end offers a challenge, as this is a tricky note to sustain. (It has a tendency to crack.) Use a strong airstream and keep your throat open and relaxed. The constant air is the key.

**Words and Music by Justin Hayward**

# Jim Horn

© Stephanie Horn

**Jim Horn**

If you think you've never heard much of Jim Horn's playing, you're wrong! According to his website, Jim Horn has played on thousands of albums to date. The credits read like a Who's Who of the music business.

James Ronald "Jim" Horn was born on November 20, 1940 in Los Angeles. He started playing piano at age seven, trumpet at nine, and then saxophone at 12. It wasn't long before he was performing professionally – at his junior high school dances and in various L.A. nightclubs. His biggest early influences were sax players King Curtis, Plas Johnson, Hank Crawford, and Clifford Scott.

When Jim was 17, he went on the road with Duane Eddy, touring for five years with the band playing sax and flute. Exposure from touring with Eddy landed Horn in the house band on TV's *Shindig!* and quickly into Phil Spector's "Wall of Sound" recording sessions. He played horns on the Righteous Brothers'

> *"After I recorded the part, [Alan Wilson] asked me to double it. I said, 'Are you sure? On a rock record?' He said yes, so we did. He liked it so much that we tripled it."*
>
> –Jim Horn on "Goin' Up the Country"

"You've Lost That Lovin' Feelin','" Tina Turner's "River Deep, Mountain High," flute and saxophone on the Beach Boys' *Pet Sounds* album, and flute on the Rolling Stones' *Goats Head Soup*. He can also boast of playing on solo albums by three members of the Beatles.

Always the busy session man, Horn toured intermittently with John Denver, between 1978 and 1993. He's released several solo albums, including 1972's *Through the Eyes of a Horn*, *Jim's Horn*, *Work It Out*, and two tribute albums: *Jim Horn: A Beatle Tributes* and *A Tribute to John Denver*, and *Northern Reflection* (2012). Most recently, he toured with Kenny Chesney.

In 2007, Horn was inducted into the Musicians Hall of Fame and Museum in Nashville as a member of the famous session band the Wrecking Crew.

Canned Heat was formed in 1966 by Alan Wilson and Bob Hite. Known for their own interpretations of blues material and firm blues roots, they got their name from Tommy Johnson's 1928 song "Canned Heat Blues." After appearances at the Monterey Pop Festival (along with Jimi Hendrix, Janis Joplin, and the Who) and headlining the Woodstock Festival at the end of the 1960s, the band acquired worldwide fame with their hits "On the Road Again," "Let's Work Together," and "Going Up the Country." This established them as one of the most popular acts of the hippie era. The band is also credited with bringing a number of other forgotten bluesmen to the forefront of modern blues, including John Lee Hooker, Sunnyland Slim, Skip James, Clarence "Gatemouth" Brown, and Albert Collins.

On September 3, 1970, Wilson died under mysterious circumstances. Hite carried on with various reconstituted versions of the band until his death in 1981, from a heart seizure. Today, remaining members, led by drummer Adolfo "Fito" de la Parra, continue to tour and record under the name Canned Heat.

# How to Play It

"Going Up the Country" (also "Goin' Up the Country") was a remake of the Henry Thomas song "Bull Doze Blues," recorded in Louisville, Kentucky in 1927. It has been called the "rural hippie anthem" and adopted as the unofficial theme song for the film *Woodstock* and the so-called Woodstock Generation. It was first released on Canned Heat's third album, *Living the Blues*, in October 1968. The song reached No. 11 on the U.S. *Billboard* Hot 100 singles chart, peaking at number 19 on the U.K. singles chart. The flute in the album version and single version differ slightly. As the band's most popular song, it continues to be used in TV commercials and movies.

There are two solos in this song – one in the introduction and the second later, using remnants of the introduction's solo. The range is fairly low in both solos, so don't hesitate to use more air to project your sound. Use a light tongue articulation and vibrato on both solos.

## Vital Stats

**Flute player:** Jim Horn
**Song:** "Going Up the Country"
**Album:** *Living the Blues*
**Age at time of recording:** 28

# Ian McDonald

The beautifully lush flute playing of Ian McDonald on "I Talk to the Wind" is surely enough to convince listeners to check out King Crimson recordings.

Ian McDonald was born on June 25, 1946 in Osterley, England. He spent his teenage years in the British army as a bandsman, where he learned clarinet and how to read music. From there, he taught himself flute and saxophone.

In 1969, he became a founding member of the progressive rock group King Crimson. The band's first album, *In the Court of the Crimson King*, reached No. 5 on the British charts and No. 28 on the *Billboard* 200 in the U.S., making it a Gold record. The album is generally viewed as one of the first works to truly embody the progressive rock genre, largely departing from the blues influences and mixing together jazz and classical symphonic elements. McDonald and drummer Michael Giles left the band and formed a spin-off group that released one album, titled *McDonald and Giles* (1971), reappearing in King Crimson in 1974.

Courtesy Photofest

**Ian McDonald**

McDonald became a founding member of the band Foreigner in 1976, playing guitar and keyboards as well as woodwinds. Throughout the '80s and '90s, he was a session musician, appearing on the hit single "Get It On (Bang a Gong)" by T. Rex, and recordings by Linda Lewis and Christine Harwood, among others. Production credits included albums by Fruupp, Darryl Way's Wolf, and Fireballet.

*Drivers Eyes*, McDonald's 1999 solo album, featured Peter Sinfield, Michael Giles, John Wetton, Steve Hackett, Gary Brooker, Lou Gramm, John Waite, and Peter Frampton. He formed the 21st

Century Schizoid Band in 2002; several tours and live albums followed.

McDonald contributed saxophone and flute to several tracks on Judy Dyble's 2009 release, *Talking with Strangers*, reuniting with former King Crimson bandmate Robert Fripp on the 20-minute "Harpsong." In 2010, Ian provided alto sax, flute, and percussion textures to *Beautiful Accident*, the debut album by progressive blues band Third International. The next year, he began working with directors of New York City's Frog and Peach Theatre Company, which specializes in off-Broadway productions and readings of Shakespeare's plays. McDonald composed and performed guitar and piano music with the group. In addition, he became involved with the band Honey West, providing lead guitar/sax/keys/harmony vocals for their live New York City performances and for their second album.

With their combination of rock, avant-garde, jazz and classical music, the group King Crimson embodied progressive rock. Deriving its name from band member Peter Sinfield's lyrics for the song "Court of the Crimson King," the band originally grew out of an unsuccessful trio called Giles, Giles & Fripp: Michael Giles (drums, vocals), Peter Giles (bass, vocals), and Robert Fripp (guitar).

Crimson made its debut at the London Speakeasy on April 9, 1969. On July 5, they played to 650,000 people at the Rolling Stones' free Hyde Park concert. In 1969, their debut album *In the Court of the Crimson King* was released. The Who's Pete Townshend endorsed it as "an uncanny masterpiece." With other albums like *In the Wake of Poseidon* and *Islands*, the group soon began an endless series of personnel changes, with only Fripp remaining through it all. Today, the band members continue to tour and record as individuals.

## How to Play It

"I Talk to the Wind" comes from the successful album *In the Court of the Crimson King*. It features a classically inspired solo in the middle of the song and a longer one at the end as a coda.

These solos may look daunting, but there are many patterns that repeat; most are just transcribed turns. Employ light vibrato on the longer notes (there aren't many), and keep the tonguing light. Work through the 16th-note passages just like you would any Mozart run, paying close attention to the classical articulations all the time. And most importantly, don't rush!

## Vital Stats

**Flute player:** Ian McDonald

**Song:** "I Talk to the Wind"

**Album:** *In the Court of the Crimson King*

**Age at time of recording:** 23

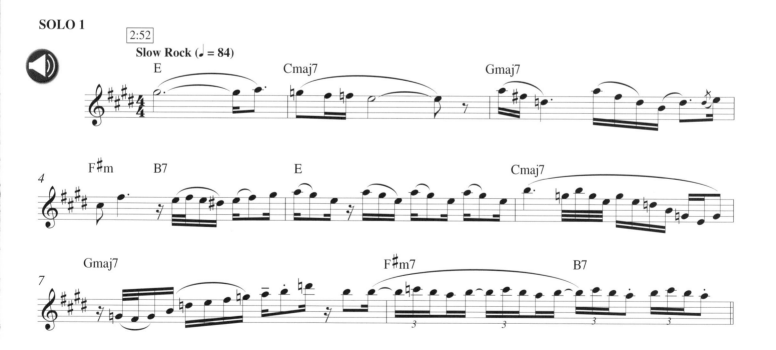

# I Talk to the Wind

*Tommy James & The Shondells*
and Cellophane Symphony

## *"It's a metaphor for the blood of Jesus."*

–Tommy James on "Sweet Cherry Wine"

"Sweet Cherry Wine" is just one of the many hits by Tommy James and the Shondells. Here, the mystery flutist provides an outstanding solo, featuring high-note prowess.

Tommy James was born Thomas Gregory Jackson in Dayton, Ohio on April 29, 1947. He was introduced to music at age three, when he was given a ukulele by his grandfather. Already a child model at age four, he took up the guitar when he was 11. At age 13, James and four of his friends from junior high school got together to play dances and parties. The group started recording singles and were noticed by Northway Sound Records. They recorded their first major single, "Judy," in 1962.

James's road to superstardom began when a nightclub DJ in Pittsburgh discovered a two-year-old record by the Shondells called "Hanky Panky" and played it at his weekend dances. It became so popular a record distributor bootlegged it, selling 80,000 copies in ten days. Tommy James and the Shondells were quickly formed, signing with Roulette Records in New York. By May of 1966, "Hanky Panky" was a No. 1 record. The album, *Hanky Panky*, went gold just four weeks after its release. James went on to record many top hits, including "I Think We're Alone Now," "Mony Mony," "Crimson and Clover," "Sweet Cherry Wine," "Mirage," "Do Something to Me," "Gettin' Together," "Crystal Blue Persuasion," and "Draggin' the Line."

In 1968, Tommy and the Shondells became one of the first acts to experiment with music videos, creating a mini-film around "Mony Mony" for theatrical showings, 13 years before MTV hit the airwaves. In 1970, the group released their *Travelin'* album, which contained the gold singles "She" and "Gotta Get Back to You." Thought by many to be the band's best work, this innovative concept album was the last LP Tommy made with the 1960s Shondells.

James became a solo artist, writing and producing the million-selling single "Tighter, Tighter" for the group Alive and Kickin'. Over the next four years, Tommy scored an additional 12 chart singles, among them "Come to Me," "Ball and Chain," "I'm Comin' Home," and "Draggin' the Line."

In 1987, pop singer Tiffany's version of "I Think We're Alone Now" and rocker Billy Idol's rendition of "Mony Mony" battled for the top spot on the pop chart for a solid month, each eventually going to No. 1. (It was the first time in music history that two cover versions of songs by the same artist went No. 1 back-to-back.) In 2010, James released his autobiography, *Me, the Mob and the Music*, which became a bestseller. It garnered rave reviews from critics and industry insiders, and was chosen by *Rolling Stone* magazine as one of the 25 greatest rock 'n' roll memoirs of all time (No. 12).

Today, Tommy James continues to tour the country and record. He has sold over 100 million records, has been awarded 23 gold singles, and nine gold and platinum albums. His songs are widely used in television and film, and have been covered by many artists.

## How to Play It

"Sweet Cherry Wine" was a Top 10 hit from the album *Cellophane Symphony* (No. 7 on the *Billboard* Hot 100, No. 6 on the Canadian charts). This song was released at the height of psychedelia, right after the group's hit "Crimson and Clover." Adding to the surreal effect of this and other songs on the album was the

## *"We were at the Hawaii and were asked if we would like to play this pig farm in upstate New York. I asked, 'What did you just say?' Finally, I said to forget about it."*

–Tommy James on passing on playing at Woodstock

then-new Moog synthesizer. The song is also a quiet protest of the Vietnam War.

The identity of the flute player remains unknown. Even James himself can't remember just who it was, stating, "It could have been any of several reed men who were working in New York then."

This solo is a great exercise in high-register notes: You'll need to know how to play all the way up to high C. (Consult a fingering chart if needed. This note isn't used often!) Keep the triplet division in your head as you play this, and place all grace notes before the beat.

The flutter-tongue technique is used in measures 2 and 7, and again on high Gs. As before, move the air more than usual and keep your throat relaxed so your tongue can "roll" freely.

## Vital Stats

**Flute player:** unknown
**Song:** "Sweet Cherry Wine"
**Album:** *Cellophane Symphony*

Words and Music by Ritchie Grasso and Tommy James

# Chris Wood

© Keystone Features / Stringer /Getty

**Chris Wood**

Chris Wood's solo on Traffic's "Freedom Rider" features some first-rate blues and jazz flute.

Chris Wood was born Christopher Gordon Blandford Wood on June 24, 1944 in Quinton, a suburb of Birmingham, England. From early childhood, he had an interest in music and painting and at age 15 taught himself how to play the saxophone. He bought a flute and started to teach himself after he was inspired by the flute playing in the movie *Jazz on a Summer's Day* in 1960. He attended the Stourbridge College of Art, called the Birmingham School of Art at that time, and was awarded a grant to attend the Royal Academy of Art,

beginning in December 1965. He soon became a busy player in several bands, including Perfect, Sounds of Blue, and – during 1965–66 – Locomotive.

Wood's younger sister was the clothes designer for the Spencer Davis Group. It was via this connection that Wood was first introduced to band member Steve Winwood. Along with Winwood, Jim Capaldi, and Dave Mason, Chris founded the band Traffic. They were first signed with Island Records. Their earliest single "Paper Sun" was released in the summer of 1967, reaching No. 5 on the U.K. charts. By the end of the year, Traffic's first album, *Mr. Fantasy*, was released.

For the most part, Wood played flute and saxophone, but occasionally performed keyboards, bass, and vocals. His most notable contribution was as co-writer, with Steve Winwood and Jim Capaldi, on "Dear Mr. Fantasy." He also played on Jimi Hendrix's *Electric Ladyland* album in 1968 and the album *The Autumn Stone* (1969) by Small Faces.

In 1970, Wood introduced the 17th-century traditional song "John Barleycorn" to the band. It became the title song of their 1970 album *John Barleycorn Must Die*. It peaked at No. 5 on the *Billboard* 200 and has been certified a gold record by the RIAA. The single "Empty Pages" spent eight weeks on the *Billboard* Hot 100, peaking at No. 74. After enlisting top session players to the line-up, Traffic toured both the U.K. and the U.S., where a live recording of their version of "Gimme Some Loving" – originally recorded by Steve Winwood's old band, the Spencer Davis Group – made the charts. Further

*"I think a lot of people came into rock 'n' roll to try to change the world. I came into rock 'n' roll to make music."*

–Steve Winwood

Traffic albums were released in the early 1970s and were big sellers: *The Low Spark of High Heeled Boys* and *Shoot Out at the Fantasy Factory*. By 1974, the band members had begun to pursue solo careers, so over time the group broke up. They reunited in 1994.

Chris Wood remained with Traffic from the time of its 1970 reformation until its 1974 breakup. While Winwood temporarily joined supergroup Blind Faith in 1969, Wood, Mason, and Capaldi teamed up with Mick Weaver – otherwise known as Wynder K. Frog – to become Mason, Capaldi, Wood, and Frog. He then went on to tour the United States with Dr. John, where he met his wife-to-be, singer Jeanette Jacobs (formerly of the 1960s girl group, the Cake).

Throughout the '70s, Chris was in demand as a session musician. His immediately identifiable flute or saxophone playing cropped up on albums by Rebop Kwaku Baah, Tyrone Downie, Fat Mattress, Gordon Jackson, Crawler, the Sky, Bobby Whitlock, and others.

Woods died of pneumonia on July 12, 1983 in Birmingham, England. He was working on a solo album at the time that was to be titled *Vulcan*. (It was released by his family in 2008.) After Wood's death, Traffic recorded one more studio album, *Far from Home* (1994). The album is dedicated to him, and the central figure on its front cover is a stick figure of a man playing flute.

The four original members of Traffic were inducted into the Rock and Roll Hall of Fame in 2004.

## How to Play It

This is a great bluesy solo that allows you to show off your technical skills. There is another opportunity to flutter tongue in measure 7, though this time it is in the middle register, which makes it a little easier. Keep the air going, as usual. In measure 15 of the original, a second flute was added to the track for a call-and-response effect (not included here).

In measures 21–22, Woods uses fast-note flurries that don't really have pitch notation, but rhythm. Just play the rhythms shown and articulate a bunch of high notes as fast as possible. Listen to the recording for ideas. It's almost impossible to notate. Also, take notice of the useful blues lick in measure 24.

## Vital Stats

**Flute** player: Chris Wood

**Song:** "Freedom Rider"

**Album:** *John Barleycorn Must Die*

**Age at time of recording:** 26

# Freedom Rider

# Collin Tilton

*"I'm not a good flute player, particularly. I think I just got lucky. I played 'Moondance' on a student model flute I paid 80 dollars for."*
–Collin Tilton

Courtesy of Collin Tilton

**Collin Tilton**

Collin Tilton displays his "jazzy side" on this Van Morrison classic, "Moondance."

Collin Tilton was born in 1946 and grew up in Trenton, New Jersey – listening to Polish music. He started playing clarinet in elementary school, and by high school had moved to the saxophone. Inspiration came from Coleman Hawkins, Lester Young, and his classically trained uncle, who lived upstairs from Tilton's family. Later finding himself at Woodstock during the heyday of the "peace and love" era, he played a number of high-profile gigs before landing with Van Morrison. With Morrison, Tilton played sax and flute lines that garnished such hits like "And It Stoned Me," "Moondance," and "Into the Mystic."

In 1978, Collin played in Etta James's band, when she was the opening act for the Rolling Stones' *Some Girls* tour. He also served as horn arranger with Clarence Clemons & the Red Bank Rockers and worked with several regional bands, notably the Shaboo All Stars. In 1989, he joined the band Eight to the Bar, and has recorded and produced the band's last eight CDs at his own Bar None Studio in North Branford, Connecticut.

To date, he is still with the band and still running the studio.

Van Morrison was born George Ivan Morrison Jr. on August 31, 1945 in Belfast, Northern Ireland. He grew listening to the blues, country, and gospel music. He became a traveling musician at 13, singing and playing guitar and sax. In 1964, he formed the band Them. Making their name at Belfast's Maritime Blues Club, the band established Morrison as a major force in the British R&B scene with hits like "Gloria," "Mystic Eyes," and "Here Comes the Night." Morrison quit the band in 1966 and went on to have a successful career as a solo artist with his first hit, "Brown Eyed Girl."

Morrison's third solo album, *Moondance*, was released in 1970. It became his first million-selling album, reaching No. 29 on the *Billboard* charts. It was rated No. 66 on *Rolling Stone's* 500 Greatest Albums of All Time. Songs like "Into the Mystic," "Crazy Love," "Domino," "Days Like This," and "Moondance" have since become pop standards, cementing Morrison as one of pop music's greatest songwriters.

With many awards, including a knighthood, six Grammys, honorary doctorates from Queen's University Belfast and the University of Ulster, and his entry into the Rock and Roll Hall of Fame in 1993, Morrison has seemingly accomplished it all.

In 2015, he released his new album *Duets: Re-working the Catalogue*, featuring singers as influential and diverse as Bobby Womack, Gregory Porter, Mavis, and Michael Bublé. The songs and re-works were chosen from Morrison's catalogue of over 360 tracks across his career. He continues to tour.

*"With "Moondance," I wrote the melody first. I played the melody on a soprano sax and I knew I had a song, so I wrote lyrics to go with the melody. That's the way I wrote that one."*

–Van Morrison

# How to Play It

"Moondance" appeared on the 1970 album of the same name, and has become Van Morrison's signature song. It was not released as a single until November 1977, seven-and-a-half years after the album was released. It reached No. 92 on the *Billboard* Hot 100. Recorded as a jazz swing number, it screams "jazz flute."

Solo 1 is the famous background flute part behind the vocals on the pre-chorus, chorus, and the verse in between. This is the famous background melody that supports the vocal line. Swing the eighth notes and use jazz articulations as written.

Solo 2 is the verse after the sax solo. There is a long tremolo between mid-register E and G (measures 9–13). Just go back and forth between E and G as fast as you can – like 16th or 32nd notes. Take a huge breath, and try to play through the five-measure phrase.

Note: Solo 2 has an unusual song form, as it is 17 measures long. Was this originally intended, or a tape splice effect? Who knows?

## Vital Stats

**Flute player:** Collin Tilton
**Song:** "Moondance"
**Album:** *Moondance*
**Age at time of recording:** 24

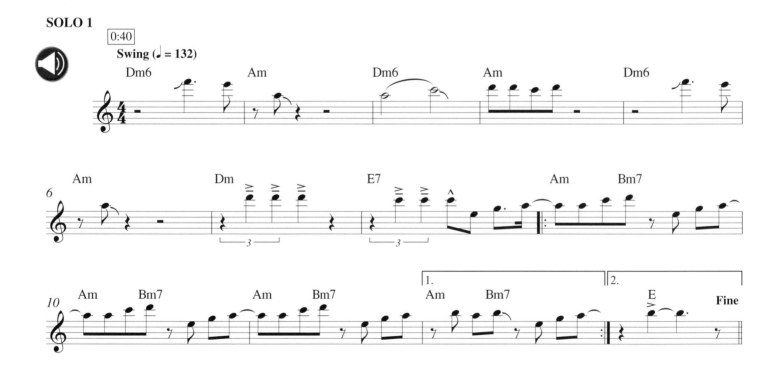

**SOLO 1**

0:40

Swing (♩ = 132)

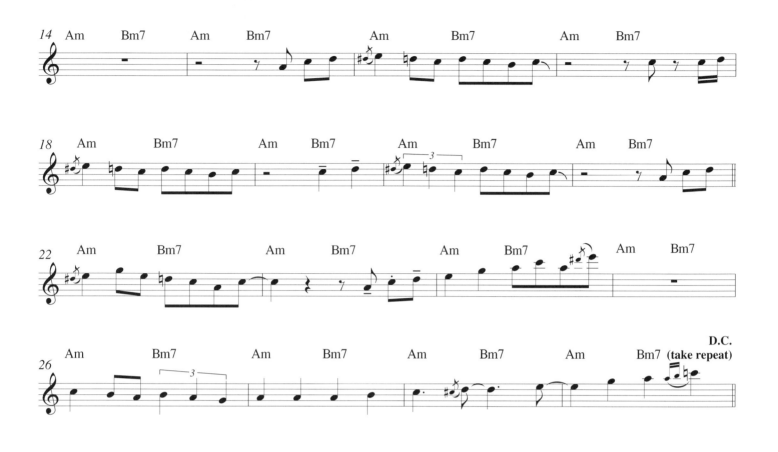

**SOLO 2**

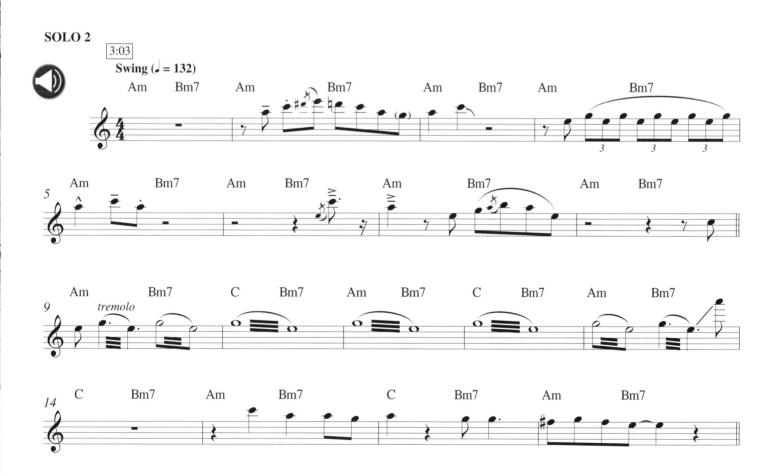

# Walter Parazaider

Saxophonist Walter Parazaider shows he can play tender flute on this popular Chicago song.

Walter "Walt" Parazaider was born on March 14, 1945 in Maywood, Illinois. Coming from a musical family, he began playing the clarinet at age nine. As a teenager, his growing talent was being groomed for a career as a professional orchestral musician. (He became the protégé of the Chicago Symphony Orchestra's E-flat clarinetist.) Walter later earned a Bachelor of Arts degree in classical clarinet performance from DePaul University. He switched to saxophone and became inspired with the idea of creating a rock 'n' roll band with horns. Forming an ensemble with friends Terry Kath, Danny Seraphine, and Lee Loughnane, the band first known as the Big Thing eventually became Chicago.

Aside from being a founding member, Parazaider's role consisted of playing woodwinds. He wrote the songs "Prelude to Aire" and "Window Dreamin,'" provided flute on "Colour My World," as well as solos on "Just You 'n' Me" and "Now That You've Gone." In 2008, he was awarded an honorary Doctor of Humane Letters by DePaul University. He continues to tour with Chicago today.

Chicago is one of the longest-running and most successful rock groups in history. They have sold over 38 million records, have 18 Platinum, 22 Gold, and 21 Top 10 singles. The band is second only to the Beach Boys in *Billboard* singles and albums chart success among American bands.

Formed of students from DePaul University and another college in 1968, the band released their first album, *The Chicago Transit Authority*, in 1969. This album included the pop hits "Beginnings" and "Does Anybody Really Know What Time It Is?" Their second album, *Chicago*, featured the hits "Make Me Smile" and "25 or 6 to 4." Their first No. 1 song was 1976's "If You Leave Me Now," which later won two Grammy Awards for Best Pop Performance by a Group and Best Arrangement Accompanying Vocalist(s) in 1977. Their 1984 album *Chicago 17* was their best-selling ever, with sensations like "Stay the Night," "You're the Inspiration" and "Hard Habit

© G. Gershoff / Getty

**Walter Parazaider**

*"I had been listening to Bach – the Brandenburg Concertos – and they had all those arpeggiated melodies. I sat at a piano and started messing around with these arpeggios. That cycle of arpeggios became the foundation of the song."*
–James Pankow on "Colour My World"

to Break." They scored another No. 1 in 1988 with "Look Away" from *Chicago 19*. Today, the band is still together after 40 years. They continue to release albums and tour to sold-out crowds.

# How to Play It

One of the band's most popular songs, "Colour My World" never charted because it was never released as a single. It was written by Chicago trombonist James Pankow, with Terry Kath singing lead vocals. The song was initially released as the B-side to "Make Me Smile" in March 1970.

Surely a singular, iconic flute solo in the pop world, this is a great study in low-to-mid-register playing. Be sure to open your embouchure, relax your throat, and send the air through the flute. Vibrato should be used on all long note values. You want to create a lyrical sound, so sing this solo in your head as you play, and think about phrasing. Tonguing should be legato throughout. Use the thumb B♭ fingering in the last phrase, alternating A and B♭.

## Vital Stats

**Flute player:** Walter Parazaider
**Song:** "Colour My World"
**Album:** *Chicago II*
**Age at time of recording:** 25

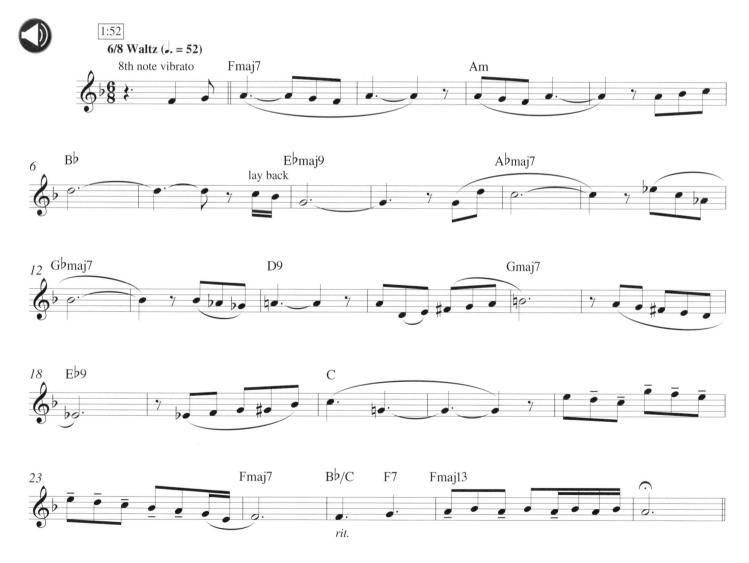

**Words and Music by James Pankow**

# Collin Tilton

> **"'Everyone' is just a song of hope. That's what that is."**
>
> –Van Morrison

See page 23 for biographical information on Collin Tilton and Van Morrison.

# How to Play It

"Everyone" is the ninth track on Van Morrison's bestselling, critically acclaimed album *Moondance*. The fastest song on the album, it's set in 12/8 time and features acoustic guitar and clavinet.

This masterful solo by Tilton shows great depth and control. It touches on every register of the flute, and is a great way to showcase range and a clear tone. Let your playing be light and carefree, and pay attention to the articulations. The first two notes of measure 12 (the 6/8 measure) should be double-tongued if possible, to keep the 16ths in tempo.

## Vital Stats

**Flute player:** Collin Tilton
**Song:** "Everyone"
**Album:** *Moondance*
**Age at time of recording:** 24

**Words and Music by Van Morrison**

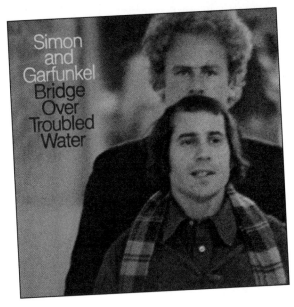

> "'So Long, Frank Lloyd Wright'… that's a wink from Simon to Garfunkel. 'So long, Artie. We'll be splitting up next year. You may not know it yet.' That's what 'So Long, Frank Lloyd Wright' is."
>
> –Art Garfunkel

Paul Simon (born October 13, 1941) and Art Garfunkel (born November 5, 1941) comprised the singing/songwriting duo Simon and Garfunkel. Attending sixth grade in Forest Hills, Queens together, they discovered their wonderful and unique sense of harmony.

Initially, they called themselves Tom and Jerry (Tom Graph and Jerry Landis) and had their first hit with "Hey, Schoolgirl," released in 1957. They went their separate ways (Garfunkel was studying architecture and Simon was studying English literature), but reunited in 1962.

Their next big song, 1964's "The Sound of Silence," was a No. 1 single in the United States and sold over a million copies. In 1966, they placed four singles and three albums in the Top 30, and soon recorded another hit song, "Mrs. Robinson," written for the soundtrack of *The Graduate*. They had huge success with their next two albums, *Parsley, Sage, Rosemary and Thyme* and *Bookends*.

*Bridge Over Troubled Water* came in 1970 and was on the charts for over a year and a half, eventually selling over 13 million copies worldwide. The album won six Grammys, including Album of the Year, Song of the Year, and Record of the Year. Around this time, Garfunkel's acting career began with roles in the movies *Catch-22* and *Carnal Knowledge*. With this development, with constant fighting between the two, and Simon's 1972 solo album, it was clear their individual solo careers were damaging the group. They split up again.

On September 19, 1981, Simon and Garfunkel teamed up to give a free concert to an estimated 500,000 fans in New York City. *The Concert in Central Park*, released the next year, went platinum. Still unable to resolve their creative differences, the two separated, performing together only occasionally.

To date, the duo has sold more than 20 million albums in the U.S. alone. Songs like "Bridge Over Troubled Water" and "The Boxer" have been listed on *Rolling Stone*'s 500 Greatest Songs of All Time. The two were inducted into the Rock and Roll Hall of Fame in 1990.

## How to Play It

Released in 1970, *Bridge Over Troubled Water* is the fifth and final studio album by Simon and Garfunkel. It was ranked No. 51 on *Rolling Stone*'s 500 Greatest Albums of All Time. Paul Simon wrote "So Long, Frank Lloyd Wright;" it was the album's fifth track. Art Garfunkel has stated that the origin of the song came from his request that Paul Simon write a song about the famous architect Frank Lloyd Wright. The lyrics have more than one meaning, as Simon has admitted the song was about Garfunkel. While Garfunkel sings the song's fadeout, producer Roy Halee can be heard on the recording calling out, "So long already, Artie!"

Much research has failed to uncover the identity of the flute soloist on this track. The excerpt features beautiful playing over the song, one with a bossa nova feel and unusual and difficult chord changes. The flute player also solos over the last minute of the song, but that material is not included here.

This is a simple solo that covers all the ranges of the flute. The articulations should be played accurately, as indicated by the accents and tenuto marks. There are pitch bends in measures 8 and 14 that can be played by rolling the head joint toward you when starting the note, then rolling the head joint back to normal position.

## Vital Stats

**Flute player:** Unknown

**Song:** "So Long, Frank Lloyd Wright"

**Album:** *Bridge Over Troubled Water*

# Curtis Amy

From the Doors to Marvin Gaye to Carol King, whenever that "Texas sound" was needed, they called Curtis Amy.

Curtis Amy was born on October 11, 1929 in Houston, Texas. He learned to play the clarinet at the early age of four. Years later, during his time in the Army, he picked up the tenor saxophone. After his tour of duty, he attended Kentucky State College and later began a teaching career in Tennessee. In his leisure time, he kept busy playing in jazz clubs. In 1965, Amy relocated to Los Angeles, where he signed with Pacific Jazz Records and released several albums: *The Blues Message*, *Meetin' Here*, *Way Down*, *Groovin' Blue*, and *Katanga!*

In addition to as leading his own bands and recording albums, Amy did session work and played solos on various recordings, including the Doors' "Touch Me," Carole King's *Tapestry* album, and Lou Rawls's album *Black and Blue*. He also worked with Dexter Gordon in the Onzy Matthews Big Band, as well as with Marvin Gaye, Tammy Terrell, and Smokey Robinson. In the mid-1960s, he spent three years as musical director of Ray Charles's Orchestra, together with his wife, singer Merry Clayton. Amy died of pancreatic cancer on June 5, 2002 in Los Angeles.

Carole King (Klein) was born February 9, 1942 in Brooklyn. She started playing piano when she was four years old. By high school, she was writing her first songs and leading a vocal quartet called the Cosines. At 17, she was singing demos for several publishers, along with her childhood friend Paul Simon. She soon became a songwriter in the now-famous Brill Building in New York City. Along with then-husband Gerry Goffin, she wrote many hits destined to become classics. Songs like "Will You Still Love Me Tomorrow?" (The Shirelles), "The Loco-Motion" (Little Eva), "Up on the Roof" (The Drifters), "I'm Into Something Good" (Herman's Hermits), and "(You Make Me Feel Like) A Natural Woman" (Aretha Franklin) have become pop standards.

As a solo artist, her biggest hit was the monster album *Tapestry*, which has sold more than 25 million copies worldwide, easily one of the bestselling albums of all time. That record sparked classic hits like "Too Late," "I Feel the Earth Move," and "So Far Away."

From 1970 to the present, King has released 25 solo albums, has won four Grammy Awards, and has had over 400 songs recorded by more than 1,000 artists. In 1987, she was given a Lifetime Achievement Award by the National Academy of Songwriters, and in 1990, she and Gerry Goffin were inducted into the Rock and Roll Hall of Fame. In 2012, she released a book of her memoirs, *A Natural Woman*.

© GAB Archive / Getty

**Curtis Amy**

*"I try to be a good person, try to write music that lifts people and makes me feel good to sing."*
–Carole King

# How to Play It

"So Far Away" appeared as the fourth single on King's 1971 *Tapestry* album. In the United States, it has been certified diamond by the RIAA, with more than 10 million copies sold. The disc received four Grammy Awards in 1972, including Album of the Year. In 2003, *Tapestry*

was ranked No. 36 on *Rolling Stone*'s list of the 500 Greatest Albums of All Time. The recording of "So Far Away" features James Taylor on acoustic guitar.

You'll want to play this laid-back pop ballad in a relaxed manner. Articulations should be soft and muted – almost slurred – throughout. Add some eighth-note vibrato on the opening A to set the mood, and play the solo like a classical etude.

## Vital Stats

**Flute player:** Curtis Amy

**Song:** "So Far Away"

**Album:** *Tapestry*

**Age at time of recording:** 42

# Tony Iommi

Who knew heavy-metal rocker Tony Iommi could play a sweet, tender flute solo when needed?

Anthony Frank "Tony" Iommi was born on February 19, 1948 in Birmingham, England. He attended Birchfield Road Secondary Modern School, where future bandmate Ozzy Osbourne was one year behind him. He initially wanted to play the drums, but as a teenager chose the guitar instead, inspired by the likes of Hank Marvin and the Shadows.

After completing school, Iommi worked for a short time as a plumber and later in a ring factory. At the age of 17, he lost the tips of his right middle and ring fingers in a sheet metal factory accident on the last day of the job. After the injury, Iommi considered abandoning the guitar entirely. But inspired by Django Reinhardt's two-fingered guitar playing, he decided to try playing again, using homemade thimbles made from melted-down plastic bottles to extend and protect his fingers.

In 1968, Tony joined forces with three of his Birmingham neighbors and school chums to form a jazz-blues band. With vocalist Ozzy Osbourne, bass guitarist Geezer Butler, and drummer Bill Ward, they first dubbed themselves Polka Salad,

eventually changing the band's name to Earth.

Over the course of time, Earth became Black Sabbath, chosen from a Boris Karloff horror film. With the new name, the band started taking a darker approach musically. Their first single was "Evil Woman," a cover of Crow's "Evil Woman (Don't Play Your Games with Me)." Their first album, *Black Sabbath*, was released in 1970, reaching No. 8 on the U.K. Albums Charts and No. 23 on the U.S. *Billboard* charts.

The band's second album, *Paranoid*, was released the next year. The songs "Paranoid," "Iron Man," and "War Pigs" become immediate rock classics and the band members were quickly propelled to superstar status. *Paranoid* became a bestseller and was a highly acclaimed album. AllMusic's Steve Huey cited *Paranoid* as "one of the greatest and most influential heavy metal albums of all time," which "defined the sound and style of heavy metal more than any other record in rock history." Ben Mitchell from *Blender* called it "the greatest metal album of all time." The album is currently ranked No. 131 on *Rolling Stone* magazine's list of the 500 Greatest

Courtesy Photofest

**Tony Iommi**

Albums of All Time, and has sold more than 75 million records worldwide.

For the next seven years, Iommi and Black Sabbath ruled the world as "the kings of heavy metal," continuing to sell millions of albums and packing arenas and stadiums. The band evolved musically through *Master of Reality* (1971), *Black Sabbath, Vol. 4* (1972), *Sabbath Bloody Sabbath* (1974), *Sabotage* (1975), *Technical Ecstasy* (1976), and *Never Say Die!* (1978). Classics songs include "Sweet Leaf," "Children of the Grave," "Changes," "Snowblind," "Sabbath Bloody Sabbath," "Symptom of the Universe," "Rock 'n' Roll Doctor," "Dirty Women," and "Never Say Die."

In 2000, Iommi released his first solo album, *Iommi*, followed by 2005's *Fused*, which featured his former bandmate

> *"I never called our music heavy metal. It was always 'heavy rock' or just 'heavy.' It's just pure power, really."*
> –Tony Iommi

Glenn Hughes. He formed the band Heaven & Hell, a heavy-metal group with Geezer Butler, along with former Black Sabbath members Ronnie James Dio and Vinny Appice. They were active between 2006 to 2010, folding after Ronnie James Dio's death in 2010.

Iommi today is widely considered one of the most influential rock guitarists of all time. A prolific riff writer, he was ranked No. 25 in *Rolling Stone* magazine's list of the 100 Greatest Guitarists of All Time. In 2011, he published his autobiography, *Iron Man: My Journey through Heaven and Hell with Black Sabbath*.

# How to Play It

"Solitude" was the seventh track on *Master of Reality*, Black Sabbath's third studio album. Released in July 1971, it was a bestseller, charting over two million copies.

The song features Iommi on piano and flute. Not much is known about his flute playing; perhaps it was an afterthought of his. He intones the simple melody in a straightforward manner, perfectly in keeping with the song's dreamlike quality.

Here's another study for playing in the low register. Maintain an open, relaxed throat and emouchure, and use enough air to project your sound. Play the excerpt with a classical flute approach, shaping the four-bar musical phrases in one breath. Add vibrato on the half notes and dotted-half notes to add to the mood of the piece. The grace notes should precede the main pulse; the principal notes should land on the beat.

## Vital Stats

**Flute player:** Tony Iommi
**Song:** "Solitude"
**Album:** *Master of Reality*
**Age at time of recording:** 23

**Words and Music by Frank Iommi, William Ward, John Osbourne and Terence Butler**
© Copyright 1971 (Renewed) and 1974 (Renewed) Westminster Music Ltd., London, England
TRO - Essex Music International, Inc., New York, controls all publication rights for the U.S.A. and Canada
International Copyright Secured
All Rights Reserved Including Public Performance For Profit
Used by Permission

# Ian Anderson

*"I'm not trying to play my instrument as if I were the guy sitting at the back of the orchestra playing flute. I'm playing it like me."*

–Ian Anderson

Flutists everywhere can thank Ian Anderson for introducing the flute into rock music – and making it cool and hip!

Ian Scott Anderson was born August 10, 1947 in Dunfermline, Scotland. He was interested in music from a young age, gaining influence from his father James's record collection of big band and jazz, as well as early rock 'n' roll by the likes of Elvis Presley. Following a traditional grammar school education, he moved on to art college to study fine art before deciding on a musical career. In 1963, alongside his school friends, he formed a band called the Blades, with Anderson on vocals and harmonica. Anderson realized he "would never be as good as Eric Clapton" and decided to sell his electric guitar to get a flute. Inspired by Rahsaan Roland Kirk (see "Soul Bossa Nova") and his album *I Talk with the Spirits*, he learned the instrument quickly.

The John Evan Band and McGregor's Engine, two blues-based local U.K. groups merged in 1968 to form Jethro Tull. Playing in a blues-rock style, Anderson's flute became the trademark sound for the basis of the band. He was the lead singer and songwriter and is often credited with bringing the flute to rock music; he also sang and played ethnic flutes and whistles, acoustic guitar, soprano saxophone, and the mandolin family of instruments.

In 1968, the band released their debut album, *This Was*, on the Island Records label, recorded only a few months after Anderson began playing flute. Jethro Tull went on to record many albums: *Benefit* (1970), *Aqualung* (1971), *Thick as a Brick* (1972), and *Living in the Past* (1972). In total, they released 30 studio

© Tom Copi / Getty

**Ian Anderson**

*"When our agent suggested the name Jethro Tull in February 1968, I, sadly, did not know who Jethro Tull was. I thought it was a name he made up. I didn't realize we were named after a historical character who invented the seed drill in the 18th century. I just fondly imagined it was some quirky name."*

–Ian Anderson

and live albums, selling more than 60 million copies

In 1983, Ian released his first of six solo albums with *Walk Into Light*. Others include *The Secret Language of Birds* (2000), the flute instrumental *Divinities* (1995), *Rupi's Dance* (2003), and *Homo Erraticus* in 2014.

He was awarded honorary Doctorates in Literature from Heriot-Watt University in Edinburgh (2006) and the Abertay University of Dundee (2010). He also received the Ivor Award for International Achievement in Music. Lately, he has toured more simply as Ian Anderson (not Jethro Tull), often with orchestras, string quartets, and featured soloists. Anderson's most recent endeavor is *Jethro Tull – The Rock Opera*.

# How to Play It

"Locomotive Breath" comes from the bestselling album *Aqualung*, released in 1971. The album has sold more than seven million units worldwide, and is Jethro Tull's best-selling album.

This solo is vintage Ian Anderson, as he hums under his playing throughout, and uses the "fat," hard tonguing he is known for. Work on humming either the same notes as the solo as you play them, or hum a drone note underneath – either will be effective. Tonguing should be harsh and hard, with double-tonguing used throughout. Make sure you always play on top of the beat.

## Vital Stats

**Flute player:** Ian Anderson
**Song:** "Locomotive Breath"
**Album:** *Aqualung*
**Age at time of recording:** 24

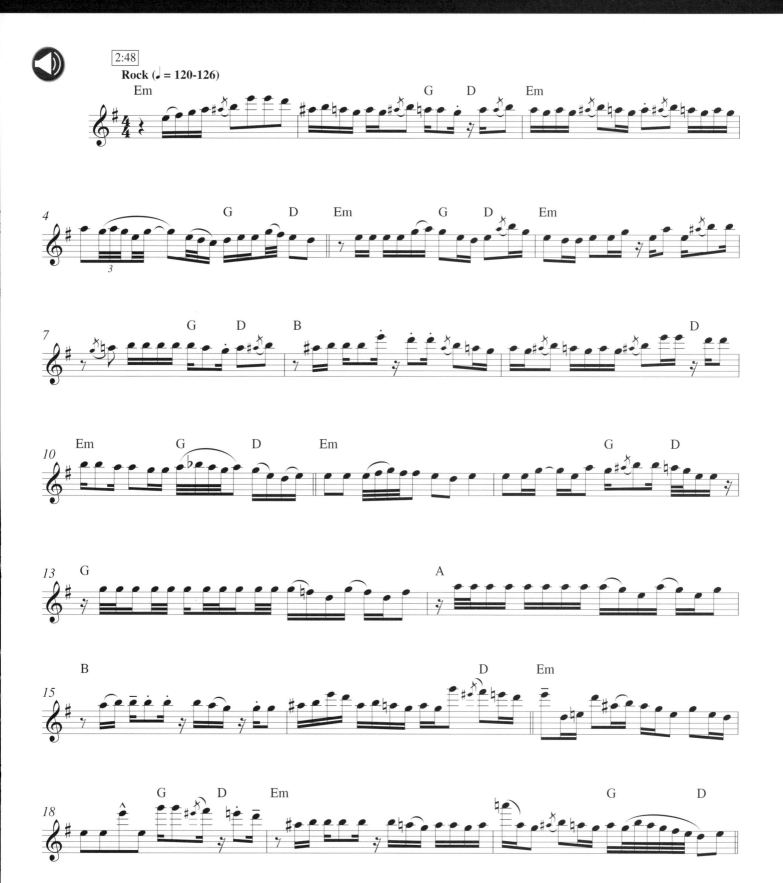

**Words and Music by Ian Anderson**

# Bob Messenger

Whenever you hear a flute, sax, or even bass on a Carpenters album, you're listening to their long-time bandmate Bob Messenger.

Robert Eugene "Bob" Messenger was born on September 30, 1935 in Pittsburg, Kansas. In the sixth grade, he began playing the clarinet given to him by his uncle Harold, later picking up the sax, flute, and upright bass. During World War II, his father, who was associated with the shipbuilding trade, moved the family to southern California. There, Bob attended Lynwood High School, graduating in 1953. He then enrolled in technical college, where he studied commercial art.

Bob moved to Los Angeles, where he played with the likes of Dick Powell, Les Elgart, Stan Worth, and the Edmond Sisters. Messenger first met Richard and Karen Carpenter in the late 1960s, just as their career was starting up. He had the good fortune to substitute for a string bass player at a club in Downey, California, where the duo was performing. At evening's end, Richard asked for his phone number, and the rest, as they say, is history. Now in his 80s, Bob continues to practice his instruments daily, plays the occasional local gig – and enjoys a challenging game of chess. He resides in Capistrano Beach, California.

The Carpenters were an American vocal and instrumental duo consisting of siblings Karen and Richard Carpenter. Famous for their soft musical style, during their 14-year career they recorded 11 albums, had 31 singles, five television specials, and a short-lived television series.

*Courtesy of Bob Messenger*

**Bob Messenger**

Richard Carpenter was born on October 15, 1946 in New Haven, Connecticut. He began listening to his father's record collection at age three, loving all styles of music. At the age of eight, he started playing the accordion, but soon switched to piano. By the time he was 15, he was studying piano at Yale and was part of a piano/bass/drums trio, playing at venues in and around New Haven. After the family moved to the West Coast, he studied piano at the University of Southern California during his senior year of high school.

Karen Carpenter was born on March 2, 1950 in New Haven, Connecticut. She began playing glockenspiel in the marching band, then turned to the drums, using a set of bar stools as her drum kit. When her parents responded by buying her a proper drum set, she was able to play it instantly. Karen was just 15 when the Carpenter Trio (Richard, Karen, and their friend Wes Jacobs) was formed.

Richard and Karen signed with A&M Records in April 1969. (Karen's parents had to co-sign for her since she was only 19 at the time.) Their first album, *Offering*, was released in October 1969, without much fanfare. But their second album, *Close to You*, skyrocketed them to fame, thanks to the singles "(They Long to Be) Close to You" and "We've Only Just Begun." "(They Long to Be) Close to You" was a No. 1 hit for four weeks in 1970, winning a Grammy Award for Best Contemporary Performance by a Duo, Group, or Chorus the next year. "We've Only Just Begun" went to No. 2. The song was No. 405 on *Rolling Stone* magazine's list of the 500 Greatest Songs of All Time, with the album ranked No. 175 on *Rolling Stone* magazine's list of the 500 Greatest Albums of All Time in 2003. They had more hit songs with "Top of the World," "Rainy Days and Mondays," "For All We Know," and "Please, Mr. Postman," and released ten albums between 1969 and 1983.

To date, the Carpenters' album and single sales total more than 100 million units. Sadly, the group ended when Karen died on February 4, 1983, of heart failure brought on by complications from anorexia.

A SONG FOR YOU

393 511-2

*"Arguably our finest album, and not just because of the many strong songs, but the arrangements, vocal work, diversity of tunes and the presentation."*

–Richard Carpenter on the album *A Song for You*

# How to Play It

"Road Ode" is track 12 on the album *A Song for You*, released on June 13, 1972. The disc has sold more than three million copies, and peaked at No. 4 on the U.S. album charts.

Messenger's brief six-bar solo is wonderful. Short and sweet, it has an easy-going feel – but with a lot of 16th notes. Keep the mood relaxed, and be careful not to crack the high E in measure 2. The tonguing in measure 5 should be legato – don't let it slow down or muddy the 16ths. Finally, add a little eighth-note vibrato on the last low E.

## Vital Stats

**Flute player:** Bob Messenger

**Song:** "Road Ode"

**Album:** *A Song for You*

**Age at time of recording:** 36

**Flute Used:** Pearl or Armstrong

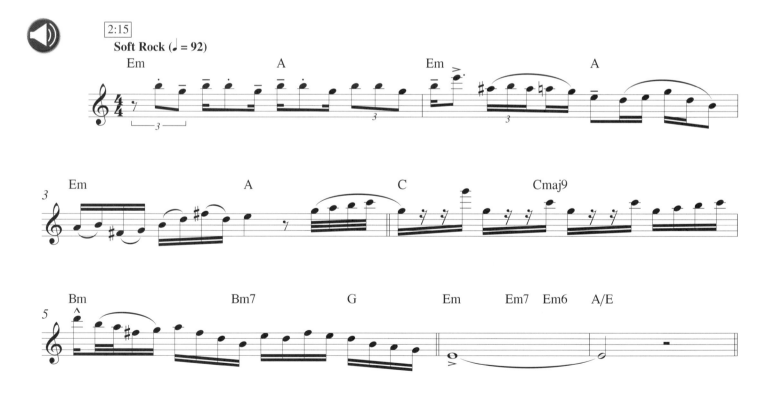

# Jerry Eubanks

*"Our success was pretty outrageous, considering the main reason we started the band in the first place was to meet chicks!"*

–Jerry Eubanks

© Tom Hill / Getty

**Jerry Eubanks**

Jerry Eubanks shows us just how to rock on a two-chord vamp!

Jerry Eubanks was born on March 9, 1950. His early musical influences were King Curtis, Aretha Franklin, and early jazz and R&B artists. He is best known as a founding member of the Marshall Tucker Band (MTB), playing saxophone, keyboards, and flute. After 25 years of touring and recording with the band, he retired in 1995.

One of the major Southern rock bands of the 1970s, the Marshall Tucker Band combined rock, country, and jazz, and featured extended instrumental passages. The band was formed in Spartanburg, South Carolina in 1971 by singer Doug Gray, guitarist Toy Caldwell, his brother

bassist Tommy Caldwell, guitarist George McCorkle, drummer Paul Riddle, and reed player Jerry Eubanks. Their name comes from a Spartanburg-area piano tuner who had rented a rehearsal space just before them. They liked the moniker and used it.

The group signed with Capricorn Records and released their eponymous debut album in 1973. It went gold by 1975. They gained recognition through a tour with the Allman Brothers Band and found significant success during the course of the '70s.

Due to constant touring, more successful albums followed: *A New Life*, released in 1974, *Where We All Belong, Searchin' for a Rainbow* (including the song "Fire on the Mountain," which peaked at No. 38 on the *Billboard* charts), and *Long Hard Ride*, the band's fifth consecutive album to go gold. In 1977, MTB released *Carolina Dreams*, which went platinum and became their most commercially successful album. The song "Heard It in a Love Song" reached No. 14 on the *Billboard* charts.

Always a busy band, they recorded a total of 17 records during the '70s and '80s under various lineups. After Tommy Caldwell was killed in an automobile accident in 1980, he was replaced by Franklin Wilke. Most of the original band members had left by the mid-1980s to pursue other projects. MTB continues to tour today, with various line-ups.

# How to Play It

"Take The Highway" is the lead song on the Marshall Tucker Band's self-titled debut album. Eubanks' solo is rocking, showing us how it's done playing on a two-chord vamp. Keep the tonguing light, and use single tongue all the way through. As the solo gets into the high octave in measure 11, be sure to keep your throat and lips relaxed on the Es and Fs, and keep the air moving. Don't tongue the Es too harshly or they might crack.

## Vital Stats

**Flute** player: Jerry Eubanks

**Song:** "Take the Highway"

**Album:** *The Marshall Tucker Band*

**Age at time of recording:** 23

*"There were a lot of unique things about the Tucker band. For one thing, Jerry Eubanks' flute put a whole different spin on a guitar-heavy sound, topping it off and riding just above the controlled chaos that was the Tucker sound."* —Charlie Daniels

**Words and Music by Toy Caldwell**

## Phil Bodner

*"'The Hustle' was a mixture of magic, timing, and good old Lady Luck. It could easily have never happened. I have to lay credit at the feet of so many."*

–Van McCoy

You can't help it! You want to slap on those disco threads and start dancing every time you hear that famous piccolo melody in "The Hustle."

Philip L. Bodner was born on June 13, 1917 in Waterbury, Connecticut. After studying music at New York University, he began working as a professional musician in New York City in the mid-1940s. Bodner played with Benny Goodman's small combo in the early 1950s, and participated in countless small group jazz recordings with fellow session stars like bassist Milt Hinton and trombonist Urbie Green. He recorded five albums for MGM while a member of the Metropolitan Jazz Quartet. As a skillful woodwind player, Phil was most active during the 1950s–'70s, recording with Frank Sinatra, Ella Fitzgerald, Mel Torme, and others.

Bodner was one of the mainstays of Enoch Light's Command label, along with Tony Mottola, Dick Hyman, Doc Severinson, and Phil Kraus, the leader of the successful now-sound instrumental group, the Brass Ring.

The Brass Ring placed two singles in the Top 40, 1966's "The Phoenix Love Theme (Senza Fine)" and "The Dis-Advantages of You" the following year. After the group disbanded in the 1970s, Bodner worked primarily as a highly sought-after session studio musician, playing saxophone and other woodwind instruments.

A favorite of Don Elliott and many other Madison Avenue jingle composers, Phil played behind hundreds of television and radio advertising spots. By 1981, as studio sessions were slowly drying up, he appeared regularly in New York City clubs as a member of a swing quartet, along with bassist George Duvivier, drummer Mel Lewis, and pianist Marty Napoleon. Bodner died on February 24, 2008 at age 90 in New York City.

Van Allen Clinton McCoy was born on January 6, 1940 in Washington, D.C. Van learned to play piano as a child and sang with the Metropolitan Baptist Church choir as a youngster.

By the time he was 12 years old, he had begun performing in local amateur shows alongside his older brother, Norman Jr., writing his own material. With his brother and a few high school buddies, Van formed a street-corner singing group called the Starlighters. McCoy was lead singer, writer, and music director for the group. They quickly moved from playing school programs and talent shows to recording their first 45rpm single, "The

**Phil Bodner**

Birdland," named for a popular dance of the late '50s. In 1958, McCoy entered Howard University to study psychology, but left after two years to begin a serious music career.

Jocko Henderson, a popular Philadelphia disc jockey, was the first to play Van's records. The two soon founded Vando Records together, and McCoy formed his own production company, VMP (Van McCoy Productions), as well. David Kapralik, A&R chief at Columbia

Records, hired Van as a songwriter with April Blackwood Music; he penned hits for Chad and Jeremy, Ruby and the Romantics, Irma Thomas, Nancy Wilson, Barbara Lewis, and others. He also put together the original Peaches and Herb duo. Impressed with Van's singing voice, Columbia Record's Mitch Miller produced an album of beautiful ballads sung by Van McCoy, *Nighttime Is Lonely Time*, released in 1966.

As a composer, McCoy wrote for Aretha Franklin, Gladys Knight and the Pips, Roberta Flack, Vikki Carr, Tom Jones, Nina Simone, Jackie Wilson, Gloria Lynn, Brenda and the Tabulations, Nat King Cole, Melba Moore, Stacey Lattisaw, David Ruffin, the Shirelles, Chris Bartley, Chris Jackson, and dozens more. He was also a frequent guest on *The Tonight Show* and on *The Mike Douglas Show*. Van's last years were spent in partnership with writer/producer Charles Kipps in McCoy-Kipps Productions. In the early '70s, he formed the Soul

City Symphony Orchestra, producing several albums, including the massive disco hit "The Hustle" in 1975. McCoy died of heart failure on July 6, 1979 in Englewood Cliffs, New Jersey. He was 39 years old.

# How to Play It

"The Hustle" by Van McCoy and the Soul City Symphony went to No. 1 on the Billboard Hot 100 and Hot Soul Singles charts during the summer of 1975, and reached No. 9 on the Australian Singles Chart and No. 3 in the U.K. The song eventually sold over one million copies and is one of the most popular songs of the disco era. "The Hustle" also won the Grammy Award for Best Pop Instrumental Performance in 1976. According to McCoy, "the dance, the hustle, was getting to be big around

the New York discos, especially with the Latinos. A friend of mine, David Todd, who DJs at Adam's Apple Disco in New York, said that whenever I get to making a disco record, I should build one around this new dance. We called it 'The New York Hustle' at the beginning, but the company shortened it."

The famous "Hustle" melody was originally played on piccolo. It's in the low range of the instrument, so not much air is needed to get the notes out. However, be sure to listen to intonation, especially on the C – it is particularly "wobbly." Keep the articulation light and enjoy.

## Vital Stats

**Flute player:** Phil Bodner
**Song:** "The Hustle"
**Album:** *Disco Baby*
**Age at time of recording:** 58

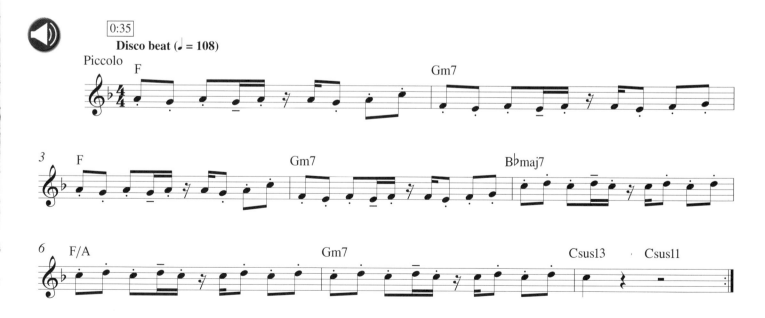

**Words and Music by Van McCoy**

# Ann Wilson

One half of the most famous sisters of rock, Heart's Ann Wilson, plays a mean flute!

Ann Dustin Wilson was born on June 19, 1950 in San Diego, California. The daughter of a colonel in the Marine Corps, Wilson and her family eventually settled in the Seattle suburb of Bellevue. Ann started playing guitar at age 12. While in high school, she added flute and sang in various groups.

After high school, she decided to devote herself to music full time. In 1970, Ann responded to a newspaper ad by a band called White Heart. They were looking for a lead singer. Thoroughly impressed by Wilson's powerful pipes, White Heart – which consisted of Steve Fossen (bass) and Roger Fisher (guitar)

at the time – immediately brought her in as lead vocalist. In 1974, her younger sister Nancy joined the band as lead guitarist, and White Heart ultimately became known simply as Heart.

With Heart, Wilson recorded a handful of albums and enjoyed a steady succession of hit songs throughout the '70s, '80s, and '90s. *Dreamboat Annie* was their debut album, released in 1975. It had the hit songs "Magic Man" and "Sing Child." Their 1977 follow-up, *Little Queen*, featured the now-classic track "Barracuda," eventually selling over three million copies. They shifted gears stylistically in 1985, to deploy a more pop-friendly sound on their eighth studio album, *Heart*. It was the band's only record to reach No. 1 in the U.S. charts, eventually selling over five million copies. It featured the hits "What About Love," "Never," "Nothin' at All," and the No. 1 song "These Dreams."

Ann had her own successes, charting with the duet "Almost Paradise" (with Mike Reno) for the soundtrack of the 1984 hit movie *Footloose*; it peaked at No. 7 on the U.S. *Billboard* pop charts. "Surrender to Me," sung with Cheap Trick lead singer Robin Zander for the soundtrack of the film *Tequila Sunrise* (1988), went to No. 6 on the U.S. *Billboard* pop radio charts.

In 1986, Wilson did the solo single "The Best Man in the World" for the soundtrack to *The Golden Child*. For the Alice in Chains' 1992 EP *Sap*, she sang vocals on the tracks "Brother," "Am I Inside," and "Love Song." That same year,

*"If you are singing rock and roll and it's 100 degrees out, then all of a sudden you have to pick up the flute and be really tender – that can be tricky."*

–Ann Wilson

Ann and Nancy formed a side band called the Lovemongers, contributing the song "The Battle of Evermore" to the soundtrack of the film *Singles*.

In 2007, Wilson released her first solo disc, *Hope & Glory*, on the Rounder record label. The album featured guest appearances from Elton John, k.d. lang, Alison Krauss, Gretchen Wilson, Shawn Colvin, Rufus Wainwright, Wynonna Judd, and Deana Carter. With Heart, Ann has sold more than 30 million records. In 2012, Heart received a star on the Hollywood Walk of Fame. They were inducted into the Rock and Roll Hall of Fame in 2013.

© Clayton Call / Getty
**Ann Wilson**

# How to Play It

"Sing Child" was the eighth track on Heart's debut album, *Dreamboat Annie*. At the time, the band was based in Vancouver, British Columbia, where it was recorded. Released in the U.S. in February 1976 through the subsidiary of Mushroom Records in Los Angeles, it was an unexpected commercial success,

peaking as high as No. 7 on the U.S. albums chart.

This solo is serious rock flute! Tongue each note hard – even overblowing sometimes to get harmonics. (Listen to Ann's original recording for an example.) The 32nd-note passage in measure 9 uses harmonic overtones for the last eight notes, marked with an x. Finger the lower octave and overblow to get the upper overtone octaves. It gives a great edgy sound and makes that passage

much easier to play in terms of fingering. But you also need much more air to get the overtones – similar to flutter-tongue air. The solo ends with Ann mirroring the guitar and fading out on an E–to–F trill.

## Vital Stats

**Flute player:** Ann Wilson
**Song:** "Sing Child"
**Album:** *Dreamboat Annie*
**Age at time of recording:** 26

**Words and Music by Ann Wilson, Roger Fisher, Steve Fossen and Dustin Wilson**
Copyright © 1976 Sony/ATV Music Publishing LLC and Andorra Music
Copyright Renewed
All Rights on behalf of Sony/ATV Music Publishing LLC Administered by Sony/ATV Music Publishing LLC, 424 Church Street, Suite 1200, Nashville, TN 37219
All Rights on behalf of Andorra Music Controlled and Administered by Universal Music Corp.
International Copyright Secured   All Rights Reserved

# Ernie Watts

Wikimedia Commons / Bob Travis

**Ernie Watts**

*"It's a melody-oriented solo, a definite part of the arrangement of the tune. It's almost more of a part itself than a strongly improvised section, but I had fun with working on making the tone beautiful."*

–Ernie Watts on "Suspicions"

Ernie Watts's beautiful flute playing proves he's more than just a master saxophonist.

Ernie Watts was born on October 23, 1945 in Norfolk, Virginia. He began playing saxophone at age 13. He won a scholarship to the Wilmington Music School where he studied classical music and technique, and was a featured soloist with the Delaware Symphony by age 16. He later won a Downbeat Scholarship to the Berklee College of Music in Boston. While a student, he began playing with drummer Buddy Rich (1966–68), recording two albums, *Big Swing Face* and *The New One.*

Watts moved to Los Angeles and began working with the big bands of Gerald Wilson and Oliver Nelson. A featured soloist on many of Marvin Gaye's original albums on Motown during the 1970s, he quickly became a first-call studio musician. Featured on over 500 recordings by artists ranging from Cannonball Adderley to Steely Dan, Aretha Franklin, and Earth, Wind and Fire to Frank Zappa (always exhibiting his unforgettable trademark sound), he could be heard on countless TV shows and movie soundtracks. That's his sax solo on Gino Vannelli's No. 4 U.S. hit "I Just Wanna Stop" (1978). In 1981, Watts toured with the Rolling Stones, appearing with them in the 1982 film *Let's Spend the Night Together.* For 20 years, he was a member of the band for *The Tonight Show with Johnny Carson,* until Carson's retirement in 1991. But

after years in the studios, Watts's passion for acoustic jazz never left him. He could frequently be heard playing fiery jazz in late-night clubs around Los Angeles.

In the mid-1980s, Watts joined bassist Charlie Haden's Quartet West, touring and recording with the group for 25 years, until Haden's death in 2014. He has released 15 albums as a leader, and has won two Grammy Awards as an instrumentalist.

Watts, in partnership with his wife Patricia, started Flying Dolphin Records in 2004. His most recent record, *A Simple Truth,* was released in 2014. Today, Watts keeps busy playing in Europe, conducting clinics and master classes, and appearing as a guest soloist with symphony orchestras.

Eddie Rabbitt was born Edward Thomas "Eddie" Rabbitt on November 27, 1941 in Brooklyn, New York. The son of Irish immigrants, his career began as a songwriter in the late 1960s. Moving to Nashville in 1968, he composed such hits as "Kentucky Rain" (1970) for Elvis Presley and "Pure Love" (1974) for Ronnie Milsap in 1974. In 1975, Rabbit signed with Elektra Records' newly established country division. In early 1976, he enjoyed his first No. 1 hit as a

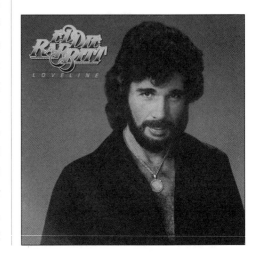

vocalist with "Drinking My Baby (Off My Mind)." Based on his strength as a songwriter, he became a successful crossover, country-influenced artist in the 1980s with such hits as "Suspicions," "Drivin' My Life Away," "I Love a Rainy Night," "Someone Could Lose a Heart," "Step by Step," and "Every Which Way But Loose." His duets "Both to Each Other (Friends and Lovers)" with Juice Newton and "You and I" with Crystal Gayle made him an even bigger star.

In the late '80s he returned to more traditional sounds, as his country shuffle "On Second Thought," from his *Jersey Boy* album (1989) demonstrates. Rabbitt was diagnosed with lung cancer in 1997 and died on May 7, 1998. His album *From the Heart* was issued posthumously.

# How to Play It

"Suspicions," from Eddie Rabbit's *Loveline* album, was originally recorded and released as a single in 1979. It went to No. 1 on the *Billboard* country music charts and to No. 13 on *Billboard* Top 100. Tim McGraw recorded a cover version on his album *Let It Go* (2007), reviving its popularity.

Ernie Watts's flute solo has so much emotion and soul, playing such perfect notes!

"Suspicions" is a beautiful piece that features the flute in two solos. In the key of A♭, the solos feature a lot of note bends and grace notes, with a repeated theme throughout both. Add eighth-note vibrato to the longer pitches, and keep the articulations light and smooth. The second solo is the outro to the song. Listen to the recording for some opportunities to "fall" off notes and "bend" into them. (Roll the head joint in or out or use your jaw to manipulate the pitch.) Double-tongue the passage in measure 11 – keep it light and ease back into single tonguing with the 16th notes that follow.

## Vital Stats

**Flute player:** Ernie Watts
**Song:** "Suspicions"
**Album:** *Loveline*
**Age at time of recording:** 35
**Flute used:** Powell Silver Flute

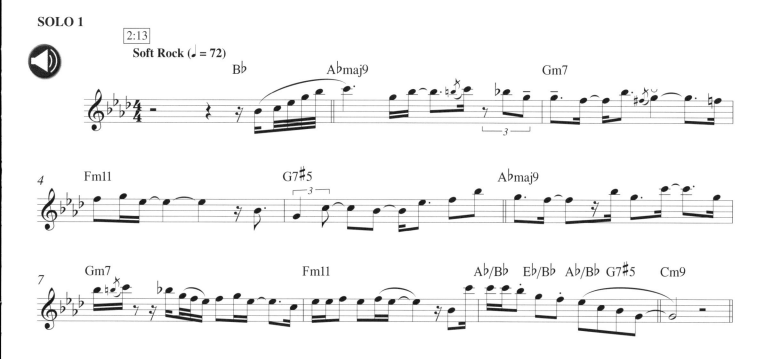

# Suspicions

**SOLO 2**

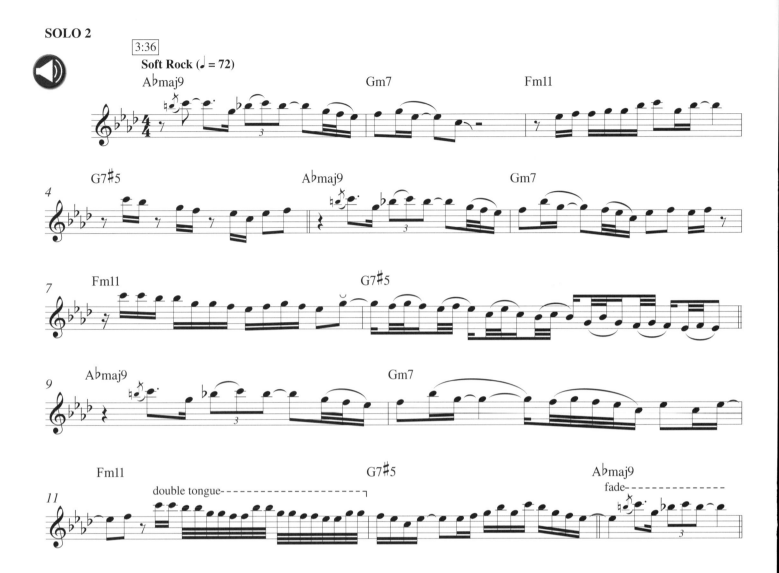

# David Shostac

*"It was the first cue of the first day of recording sessions, led by John Barry. I had no idea it would become a classic!"*

–David Shostac on "Somewhere in Time"

The *Somewhere in Time* theme has to be – hands down – one of the most beautiful movie melodies ever written. And flutist David Shostac deserves half the credit!

David Shostac was born on July 17, 1941 in Los Angeles. Both his parents were musicians. Starting flute at age eight, David graduated *cum laude* from Occidental College and earned a master's degree from Juilliard, where he studied with Julius Baker. He's been principal flutist of the St. Louis, Milwaukee, and

**David Shostac**

New Orleans Symphony Orchestras, as well as the Mostly Mozart, Ojai, Carmel Bach Festival and Aspen Chamber Orchestras. In addition to his long tenure with the Los Angeles Chamber Orchestra, he has performed as principal flutist with the Aspen Festival Orchestra for 15 years.

Shostac has played on hundreds of film soundtracks, including *Somewhere in Time, Avatar, A Beautiful Mind, Troy, Life of Pi, The Little Mermaid,* and *Pearl Harbor.* He has worked with composers like John Williams, Jerry Goldsmith, James Horner, John Barry, and Alexandre Desplat.

Previously on the faculties of USC, UCLA, UC Irvine, the Aspen Music School, and the California Institute of the Arts, he currently teaches at California State University at Northridge and the Henry Mancini Institute. His book, *Super Warmups for the Flute* (1992), is popular with students, teachers, and professionals.

Composer John Barry was born John Barry Prendergast on November 3, 1933 in York, England. He spent his early years in cinemas his father owned, where he quickly grew to love film music. His mother was a talented pianist. Early on, he showed an avid interest in studying piano, but switched to the trumpet in his teens. After completing his national service in the British Army, assigned to a musical unit, he formed his own band in 1957, the John Barry Seven. Before long, he developed an interest in composing and arranging, making his debut for television in 1958.

In 1960, Barry was invited to write his first film score, *Beat Girl*, starring Adam Faith. He soon started his film composer legacy with the first James Bond movie, *Dr. No*, going on to compose the soundtracks for 11 of the James Bond films, between 1963 and 1987.

He received many laurels for his work, including five Academy Awards: two for *Born Free* and one each for *The Lion in Winter* (for which he also won the first BAFTA Award for Best Film Music), *Dances with Wolves*, and *Out of Africa*. (The latter two also garnered Grammy Awards for Barry.) He received ten Golden Globe Award nominations, winning once for Best Original Score for *Out of Africa* in 1986. Barry completed his last film score, *Enigma*, in 2001 and recorded the successful album *Eternal Echoes* the same year. In 1998, he was inducted into the Songwriters Hall of Fame, and made a Fellow of the British Academy of Film and Television Arts in 2005. Barry died of a heart attack on January 30, 2011 in Glen Cove, New York.

# How to Play It

The *Somewhere in Time* melody is one of the most famous and beautiful film melodies ever written. Used for wedding processionals (this writer's included), it has turned out to be a symbol of romance and love. Although a box office disappointment in the United States, the film *Somewhere in Time* (1980) was a huge hit in Asia, becoming one of the highest-grossing films in China.

The music soundtrack is Barry's all-time bestselling score, outpacing all his other soundtracks combined. He wrote the music after the death of his parents. Actress Jane Seymour, a longtime friend of the Barrys and star of *Somewhere in Time*, offered to help get him involved as composer, since he was not the producers' original choice. For the first time in his career, Barry accepted a percentage of soundtrack sales, which was a successful move; the soundtrack still sells well throughout the world.

Classically trained Shostac plays this melody as beautifully as one might imagine. Surely the song's popularity owes something to his classic rendition.

Although performed and recorded on alto flute on the original, C flute was used for this book's recording. (Since low A doesn't exist on a C flute, that note is omitted in the recording.) On the soundtrack recording, the flute plays the first eight bars as a solo, then the violins take up the melody. For the purposes of this book, the entire song melody is presented.

Pay close attention to your tone and vibrato on this solo. The timbre should be warm and full, with a wide eighth-note vibrato – as if you are singing the melody. Breathe where marked to keep the phrases together. Finally, use plenty of warm air and a relaxed jaw to project your sound in this low register.

## Vital Stats

**Flute player:** David Shostac

**Song:** "Somewhere in Time"

**Album:** *Somewhere in Time* soundtrack

**Age at time of recording:** 39

**Flute used:** Muramatsu silver-plated alto flute (modeled after Julius Baker's Powell alto flute)

# Somewhere in Time

# Greg Ham

Courtesy Photofest

**Greg Ham**

Greg Ham is known for his signature licks on 1980s hits like "Who Can It Be Now?" and "Down Under" from the band Men at Work.

Gregory Norman Ham was born on September 27, 1953 in Melbourne, Australia. During his teen years, he was a popular actor in school plays. In 1972, Greg met future bandmate Colin Hay, and in 1979 joined the original lineup of the band Men at Work.

As a multi-instrumentalist, Ham played saxophone, keyboards, flute, and harmonica for the group, as well as singing vocals. He performed the saxophone solo on the song "Who Can It Be Now?" (a rehearsal take that was used in the final mix) and improvised the flute riff in the song "Down Under." In June 2009, music publisher Larrikin Music sued Men at Work and their record label EMI for plagiarism, alleging that the flute riff copied the 1934 nursery rhyme "Kookaburra," to which they owned the publishing rights. The Federal Court of Australia ruled that "Down Under" did infringe the copyright of "Kookaburra Sits in the Old Gum Tree" and awarded Larrikin five percent of the song's royalties, backdated to 2002. Several appeals by EMI and Men at Work were unsuccessful. Ham said he was deeply affected by the judgment and felt it had tarnished his reputation.

In addition to Men at Work, Ham played brass and keyboard in the R&B band Relax with Max. The lineup consisted of front man Max Vella, Linda "Toots" Wostry on saxophone, James Black on keyboard, David Adam and Ross Hannaford on guitars, and John James "JJ" Hackett on drums. They played at the Metropol in Fitzroy-Melbourne, Australia, and on ABC's television comedy *While You're Down There*. The band also backed several Australian artists, including Kylie Minogue, as well as American soul singers James Brown and Bo Diddley. After leaving Men at Work in 1985, Ham reunited with the band in 1996 for a tour of the United States. In his final years, he taught guitar at Carlton North Primary School and assessed music students for the Victorian Certificate of Education. Ham died at age 58 on April 19, 2012 in Carlton North, Melbourne from a heart attack.

The Australian group Men at Work formed in 1978. Their founding mainstay was Colin Hay on lead vocals, forming the group with Jerry Speiser on drums and Ron Strykert on lead guitar. They were later joined by Greg Ham on flute and keyboards and John Rees on bass guitar. In January 1983, they were the first Australian artists to have a simultaneous No. 1 album and No. 1 single on the United States *Billboard* charts: *Business As Usual* and "Down Under." Their second album, *Cargo*, went No. 1 in Australia, No. 2 in New Zealand, No. 3 in the U.S., and No. 8 in the U.K. They had other hit singles, including "Who Can It Be Now?" (No. 2, Australian charts; No. 1, U.S.), "Overkill" (No. 3,

*"I'm terribly disappointed that that's the way I'm going to be remembered – for copying something."*

–Greg Ham on the "Down Under" controversy

MEN AT WORK

BUSINESS AS USUAL

U.S.), "It's a Mistake" (No. 6, U.S.) and "Be Good Johnny" (No. 8, Australia). The band won the Grammy Award for Best New Artist of 1983 and has sold more than 12 million records. The group disbanded in 1986 and reunited in 1996, only to disband again by 2002.

# How to Play It

Men at Work recorded and released "Down Under" (also known as "Land Down Under") in 1980, as the B-side to their first local single "Keypunch Operator." Released before the band signed with Columbia Records, it was written by the group's co-founders, Colin Hay and Ron Strykert. The best-known version was released in October 1981, as the third single from their debut album, *Business as Usual*. The song went to No. 1 in their native Australia in December 1981, and No. 1 in the U.S. in January 1983. It eventually sold over two million copies in the U.S. alone. It has since become a popular and patriotic song in Australia.

The song riff and solo are the most recognizable parts of the song.

Solo 1 is the famous opening flute lick by Ham. Beat 2 of measures 1 and 3 is a mordent on B leading into A (B-C♯-B A). Keep it in time and be sure to end on A on the "and" of 2. Double-tongue the first beat of measure 4 to keep it light and even.

Solo 2 features a run from low F-sharp to high D – just play as many notes in between as you can (slurred) and end on the D on beat 2. Double-tongue again on beat 1 of measures 4 and 8. Finally, work out the 16th-note triplets in measure 6 so they are clean and even. They should sound like a flourish of notes, but if you divide them into groups of three, you can get them all.

## Vital Stats

**Flute player:** Greg Ham
**Song:** "Down Under"
**Album:** *Business as Usual*
**Age at time of recording:** 28

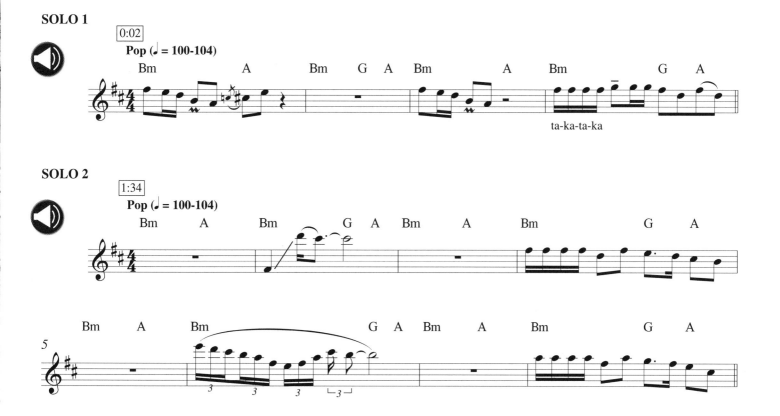

## Björn J:son Lindh

*"One night in Bangkok and the world's your oyster. The bars are temples, but the pearls ain't free."*

–Lyric from "One Night in Bangkok"

Courtesy Tapperheten / Wikipedia

**Björn J:son Lindh**

We might consider "One Night in Bangkok" the ethnic solo of this book, due to its Southeast Asian flavor and content.

Björn J:son Lindh was born on October 25, 1944 in Arvika, Sweden. He started his music education at Ingesund College of Music in Arvika in 1962. Between 1963 and 1971, he studied both piano and flute at the Royal Swedish Academy of Music (today the Royal College of Music) in Stockholm. Lindh began his professional career as a pop musician during the 1960s with the group Atlantic Ocean. In the 1970s, he became an active studio musician.

Lindh's first solo album, *Ramadan*, was released in 1971 – under the name Jayson Lindh in the U.S. He composed chamber music, symphonic works, concertos for various instruments, choral music, and scores for feature films such as *Mannen på taket (Man on the Roof)*

and *Jägarna (The Hunters)*. He played on several of Swedish electronic music composer Ralph Lundsten's albums during the 1970s and 1980s. His first U.S. solo release, *A Day at the Surface*, was recorded at Sonet Records in Stockholm in 1978. Though Lindh was a flutist, he frequently performed on the piano (or Fender Rhodes), and made use of various synthesizers on many of his recordings. He released about 30 solo albums during his career; "Brusa högre lilla å" ("Sing Louder, Little River") is probably his best-known piece of music. J:son was also a session musician for ABBA, Chess, Gardestad, Schaffer, Vreeswijk, Oldfield, Hazelwood, Törnell, et al. He made a series of solo albums with guitarist Jan Schaffer and later with classical pianist Staffan Scheja.

In 1984, Lindh played the flute solo on Murray Head's U.K. No. 1 single "One Night in Bangkok." He collaborated in 1986 with the progressive New Age music group Triangulus on their self-titled album. In the '90s, Lindh created graphic art using copper ink, ink, watercolor, and acrylic paint; it was shown in several exhibitions. He performed many times together with his wife, organist Marie J:son Lindh Nordenmalm, in the Church of Nora (Sweden), where he was active until his death on December 21, 2013. He died of a brain tumor.

Murray Head was born March 5, 1946 in London, England. His mother and father were both involved in film. Head appeared in his father's documentaries at the age of seven, and began his performing career at age 12 with appearances in several radio plays. He started writing songs a year later and, at 16, ran away from home to seek out a recording career in London. He eventually released some singles under the supervision of famed producer Norrie Paramor. In 1966, he made his film debut in *The Family Way*, which featured his song "Some Day Soon," produced by Tim Rice. Still, Murray's musical pursuits failed to take off and he was eventually dropped from his recording contract; he spent a few years selling insurance.

His career was resurrected when Rice and composer Andrew Lloyd Webber contacted him to sing the role of Judas on the soundtrack to their musical *Jesus Christ Superstar*. Head next appeared in the film *Sunday Bloody Sunday* (1971). The success of both these movies

CHESS

BENNY ANDERSSON     TIM RICE     BJÖRN ULVAEUS

launched Murray to mainstream attention and, in 1972, he recorded his debut solo album *Nigel Lived*. Apart from a starring role in 1977's *The French Woman*, he spent the remainder of the decade out of the spotlight, finally returning in 1980 with two more albums, *Voices* and *How Many Ways*.

In 1984, Murray was tapped to star in the musical *Chess*, with his soundtrack performance of "One Night in Bangkok" released as a single. It became a major pop hit on both sides of the Atlantic. In 1999, he co-wrote the screenplay to *The Children of the Century* and returned to the stage in 2003 in the musical *Cindy* in Paris. Today, he continues to keep busy acting.

# How to Play It

"One Night in Bangkok" comes from the Tim Rice/Benny Andersson/Björn Ulvaeus musical *Chess*. The music was composed by former ABBA members Benny Andersson and Björn Ulvaeus, with lyrics by Rice and Ulvaeus. The verses were sung/spoken by Michael Head, with Swedish singer and songwriter Anders Glenmark singing the choruses.

It became a U.K. No. 1 single, also topping the charts in many countries, including South Africa, West Germany, Switzerland, and Australia. It peaked at No. 3 in both Canada and the United States in May 1985.

The solo by Lindh uses flutter tongue in the first four measures – but in the low register, so it won't require as much air. An Arabian scale adds an ethnic flavor all the way through. This excerpt also uses the flute's first trill key (the key between first and second finger on right hand) throughout the solo, as notated in the music. Use harmonic overtones in measures 8 and 9 to get that edgy sound on the Ds. (Finger the low register D while overblowing to get the middle register.) Finally, tongue the last four notes while moving your jaw up and down quickly to get a "scoop" effect.

## Vital Stats

**Flute player:** Björn J:son Lindh
**Song:** "One Night in Bangkok"
**Album:** *Chess*
**Age at time of recording:** 40

**Words and Music by Benny Andersson, Tim Rice and Bjorn Ulvaeus**

# Katisse Buckingham

© Ian Barling

**Katisse Buckingham**

Los Angeles musician Katisse Buckingham has assured his place in cinema history with his virtuosic flute solo from the hit movie *Anchorman: The Legend of Ron Burgundy*.

Katisse Buckingham was born on August 28, 1971 in Los Angeles. Both his parents were musicians and music was always played in the house. He started out as a child actor and model, picking up the saxophone at age 12. He attended the Los Angeles County High School for the Arts as a theatre major, further developing his love for spoken

word, poetry, and rhyme schemes. Miles Davis, Run DMC, and Weather Report were early music influences. Buckingham received an NEA Jazz Fellowship Grant, attending college at the Grove School of Music, where he studied extensively with woodwind master Bill Green and composer Rob McConnell. He also attended the National Music Camp in Interlochen, Michigan, and won the L.A. Jazz Society's New Talent Award. He started playing the flute at age 18.

Playing tenor, alto, and soprano saxophones, C flute and alto flute, he was featured on the Golden Globe winning score to the Robert Redford film *All Is Lost* and on the Universal Pictures animated film *Minions* (2015), as well as *Anchorman: The Legend of Ron Burgundy*.

Today, Katisse is one of Los Angeles's most seasoned and versatile musicians, performing and/or recording with the Yellowjackets, Prince, Billy Childs, Dr. Dre, Herbie Hancock, Roy Ayers, Andy Summers, Zawinul Legacy Band, Airto & Flora Purim, the Los Angeles Guitar Quartet, John Daversa Small Band, Colin Hay, Poncho Sanchez, Don Grusin, Lionel Richie, Pete Yorn, Alan Ferber Big Band, Full Time Fools (with Jimmy Haslip, Otmaro Ruiz, Luis Conte, and Jimmy Branly). He also leads his own groups, such as the Oddsemble.

Alex Wurman is a highly versatile award-winning composer with a broad musical palette. Hailing from Chicago, he comes from a family of generations devoted to the study and performance of music. He attended the prestigious Academy of Performing Arts High School, later studying composition at the University of Miami in Coral Gables and at the American Conservatory of Music in Chicago. After college, Wurman

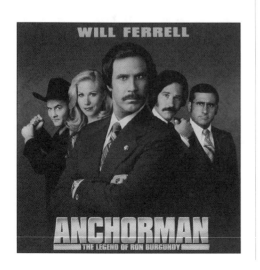

> *"It was two pages of chord changes and that's it. No melodies written. "Aqualung" was part of the scene already, so I just played that bit."*
>
> –Kattise Buckingham

moved to Los Angeles to pursue a career in film scoring.

Movie scores include his eerie piano melodies of *Confessions of a Dangerous Mind*, minimalist/20th-century sculpted sounds in *Temple Grandin*, groovy '70s themes for *Anchorman: The Legend of Ron Burgundy*, contemporary interpretations of French Impressionism for *Thirteen Conversations About One Thing*, and soulful melodies combined with ethereal orchestrations for *March of the Penguins*. He also wrote the score for the wildlife documentary *The Last Lions,* directed by Dereck Joubert, which garnered his second award for "Best Music" at the world's leading natural history film forum, the Jackson Hole Wildlife Film Festival. Though known primarily for his work on films, he won the Emmy for Outstanding Music

## Vital Stats

**Flute player:** Katisse Buckingham

**Song:** movie scene from *Anchorman: The Legend of Ron Burgundy*

**Album:** not available on original soundtrack

**Age at time of recording:** 33

**Flute used:** Yamaha YFL-892 with Yamaha CY solid 14k gold head joint

Composition for a Miniseries, Movie, or Special for HBO Films' *Temple Grandin*.

# How to Play It

The film *Anchorman: The Legend of Ron Burgundy* was released on July 9, 2004 and grossed $85,288,303 in North America, for a worldwide total of $90,574,188. The film opened at No. 2 in its first weekend, behind *Spider-Man 2*. The sequel, *Anchorman 2: The Legend Continues*, was released on December 18, 2013.

By far the hardest excerpt of the bunch, this solo requires dexterity, control, and high-note chops. Warning: This is not for the faint of heart.

This solo features every technique, style, and flute control possible. Between the flutter tongues, falls, high-note facility and technique, practice it slowly and in small segments. It was never released on the soundtrack, so watch the movie, or search online for this famous segment of the movie.

Katisse starts the solo all by himself, with a rapid ascending pattern that quickly reaches a high A♯ before blurring down to the E. Just play as many notes between the high A♯ and the low E on beat 1 of measure 2 as possible. The flutter-tongue in measure 8 kicks off the next section. Be sure to double-tongue in measure 9.

The jazz swing section begins at measure 14, leading into one of the hardest lines in this solo in measures 19–20. Practice slowly and use tons of air on the high notes with a controlled, but not too strained, embouchure to keep the notes from cracking.

Measure 24 turns into double-time fast swing. Double-tongue from measures 24–30 to get all the notes in! Measures 32–37 are not really in perfect time with the rhythm section, so just read the part as is. (The nearly inaudible track from the movie makes these measures difficult to transcribe.)

"Stop time" happens at measure 38; the rhythm section drops out. Be sure to hum while playing the Ds and use twice the air you normally do to accomplish this, for that "growl" effect. With the tempo so fast and no rhythm section (and an inaudible rhythm track), timing and accurate notation was difficult. Between measures 54–60 Katisse is slowly doing a chromatic ascend. Make sure you move chromatically up the flute, landing on the notated beats and notes.

Measure 62 quotes the famous flute line and melody "Aqualung" (see Ian Anderson) before doing some serious high-note passages with fast double tonguing. Practice slowly and be sure not to tense up. Finally, measure 65 features a scoop into high A (while humming, of course), before ending on an impressive super-high E. (You'll need to look up the fingering for this one.). Have a blast with this crazy solo!

Note: Watch this clip on YouTube repeatedly to get it in your head. The transcription doesn't do it full justice.

**By Marc Ellis**
Copyright © 2004 Songs Of SKG
All Rights Administered by Sony/ATV Music Publishing LLC, 424 Church Street, Suite 1200, Nashville, TN 37219
International Copyright Secured   All Rights Reserved

# About the Author

**Eric J. Morones** hails from Racine, WI. He attended the University of Wisconsin-Whitewater, where he received a degree in communications. He later did graduate work in jazz studies at the University of North Texas. Now living in Los Angeles, Eric has played, toured, and/or recorded with Kelly Clarkson, the Brian Setzer Orchestra, Big Bad Voodoo Daddy, Drake Bell, Bobby Caldwell, Steve Tyrell, Maureen McGovern, Jack Sheldon, Bill Holman, Will Kennedy, and Chad Wackerman. His sax playing is featured on the *Big Fish Audio Sample DVD Suite Grooves 1 and 2*. He has performed at the Montreux and North Sea Jazz Festivals, as well as on *The Tonight Show with Jay Leno, Dancing with the Stars, Late Night with Conan O'Brien, The Today Show, Live with Regis and Kelly*, and *Woodstock '99*.

A busy author, Eric has written the books *101 Saxophone Tips, Paul Desmond Saxophone Signature Licks, 25 Great Saxophone Solos, 25 Great Trumpet Solos*, and *Saxophone Workout* (Hal Leonard Publishing). He wrote a bi-monthly column for the *Saxophone Journal* called "From the Front Lines," and produced two Masterclass CDs for the magazine: *How to Play Pop, R&B and Smooth Jazz* and *How to Play the Blues*. Eric's first solo jazz CD, *About Time!*, is available on Arabesque Records.

ericmorones.com